IT'S WHO
WE ARE

JAMES J. HOLDEN
FOUNDER, MANTOUR MINISTRIES

IT'S WHO WE ARE
Copyright © 2023 Mantour Ministries

Published by 4One Ministries, Inc. Visit www.mantourministries.com for more information on bulk discounts and special promotions, or e-mail your questions to info@4oneministries.org.

Design: James J. Holden

Subject Headings:
1. Christian life 2. Men's Ministry 3. Spiritual Growth

ISBN 978-1-7378821-6-9
ISBN 978-1-7378821-8-3 (ebook)
Printed in the United States of America

DEDICATION

In life, we are blessed to meet people from all walks of life. I have been blessed with many friendships, and I want to dedicate this book to one friend in particular. This friend has demonstrated the ability to overcome many obstacles and hindrances in life. He has gone from being the youngest person to graduate from a Teen Challenge Center to becoming a pastor, a leader of young adults, a member of the Mantour Ministries/4One Ministries Board of Directors, and an incredible man of God.

I am so proud of him. I watch him with his young children and marvel at how amazing a father he is as he lovingly, patiently, and gently takes care of them and shows them a godly example. His heart for God and his family is truly impressive.

I am thankful for his support and his friendship, and I am happy to dedicate this book to my spiritual brother, Joey Cullen.

TABLE OF CONTENTS

1. WHO ARE YOU 7

2. CREATED, NOT EVOLVED 17

3. HEIRS, NOT SLAVES 29

4. WARRIORS, NOT WIMPS 41

5. LEADERS, NOT RULERS 55

6. PURE, NOT POLLUTED 67

7. FOLLOWERS, NOT FANS 79

8. VICTORS, NOT VICTIMS 91

9. DOERS, NOT HEARERS 101

10. COACHES, NOT COMPETITORS 111

11. INFLUENCERS, NOT INFLUENCED 123

12. IT'S WHAT WE DO 133

WORKBOOK 137

BIBLIOGRAPHY 165

CHAPTER ONE
WHO ARE YOU?

I love the ministry God has called me to do! It is the realization of a lifelong dream of ministering to men. As part of the ministry (and because I live in the boonies), I spend A LOT of time in the car traveling. These many hours in the car yield a lot of radio time.

Often I listen to music. Sometimes I'll listen to sports talk radio. My third go-to has become podcasts, especially during a long drive home after a conference. I can focus more on a podcast, which keeps my mind alert when my body wants to sleep.

While I wish that I could be super-spiritual and say that I always listen to sermons or Christian teaching podcasts, the truth is that I don't. I often listen to fantasy football podcasts or other topics of enjoyment. One of my favorite podcasts right now is *Pod Meets World*. I know, that really shows my age!

Still, I enjoy turning my brain off for a few moments and relaxing while the hosts reminisce about the lives of *Cory, Sean, Eric,* and

Topanga from the hit 90s TV show, *Boy Meets World*. While I don't usually agree with their political views, that's a tiny portion of the show, and it's fun to hear the behind-the-scenes stories as they rewatch the episodes of this nineties TV show.

Of course, being a writer and a minister, I often find that my brain still finds inspiration even when I'm trying to relax and turn off my mind. This happened one day while we were riding in the car listening to a *Pod Meets World* episode.[1] In this episode, they interviewed Adam Scott, who played *"Griff"* in Season Two.

"Griff" (as he was called on the show) told the story of coming in mid-season to replace *"Harley Keiner."* He said he was really nervous, but he quickly made friends with the guys who played *"Joey"* and *"Frankie."*

Still, they couldn't resist playing pranks on the new guy.

One day, after *"Griff"* told *"Joey"* and *"Frankie"* (I'm just going to call them by their character names) a really filthy, dirty joke, *"Joey and Frankie"* said, *"Oh, man, you know who would love that joke—the guy who plays 'Mr. Turner'".*

Now, here's where things get interesting: Almost immediately, the show's hosts (the now adults who then played *Topanga, Sean,* and *Eric*) began saying, *"Oh no! Not him!! You can't tell HIM that joke! No!"*

And that was the prank. Apparently, the man who played *"Mr. Turner"* was a very conservative Christian. Everyone on the set knew him as a man with beliefs guiding his life. Everyone knew he'd never laugh at the joke, and the new guy would feel foolish.

Of course, everyone wanted to know what happened when *"Mr. Turner"* heard the joke.

Just as they expected, he didn't laugh. Instead, he said, *"Wow! It seems like the guy in that story could use a lot of help."*

Hearing the response, the hosts said, *"Yep, that's who he was."*

The best part was that they loved him for it. Even those who were not Christians or even religious still had tremendous respect for this man who knew what he believed and always lived by his beliefs. They credit him as someone they trusted, felt safe around, and still love his friendship. They often talk about his tremendous sense of humor and the inside jokes they all shared.

Listening to this podcast, I started thinking, *"What an incredible testimony. They knew he was a Christian. They knew he was conservative. They knew he stood by his beliefs and knew he'd live what he believed."*

It also struck me that the man who played *"Mr. Turner"* could be a witness for Christ in his environment without being a jerk about it.

He was their friend. He was their co-worker. They loved being around him and laughing with him, but they knew... He's a Christian. And they respected that.

It was just who he was.

Guys, who are you?

> IT IS VITAL IN TODAY'S WORLD FOR MEN TO TRULY UNDERSTAND THEIR IDENTITY, ESPECIALLY THEIR IDENTITY IN CHRIST.

What would people say your identity is? What characteristics in your life stand out the most to other people? What would they say about you if they described you and said, *"It's Who You Are"*?

I think it is vital in today's world for men to truly understand their identity, especially their identity in Christ. We live in a world desperately trying to redefine everything, especially men.

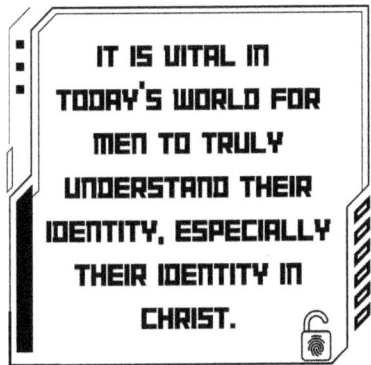

The world is trying to redefine manhood and destroy men, predominantly Christian men. They are trying to get you to think differently, act differently, and cower in the corner. They honestly see little use for men.

We live in a society that demonizes men and blames them for everything wrong in the world. Masculinity is called toxic. The woke agenda wants to destroy all institutions built on male patriarchy. In today's world, men are the enemy.

Daily, society is bombarded by a micro-minority trying to make their way of life seem normal, superior, and desirable. They are trying to change the identity of a man—especially a man of God.

That is why now, more than ever, we need to know our identity. We need to know who we are in Christ. Amidst all the attacks, we have forgotten the three P's of our godly identity: our power, privilege, and protection.

What do I mean? Let's look briefly at each one.

1. Our Power

As men of God, we have unlimited spiritual power at our disposal. We need to know and understand this power to survive the attacks on our identity around us.

The Bible tells us what power we have as Spirit-filled believers.

> *If the Spirit of him who raised Jesus from the dead dwells in you, he who raised Christ Jesus from the dead will also give life to your mortal bodies through his Spirit who dwells in you. Romans 8:11*
>
> *...you will receive power when the Holy Spirit has come upon you. -Acts 1:8*
>
> *I will give you the keys of the kingdom of heaven, and*

whatever you bind on earth shall be bound in heaven, and whatever you loose on earth shall be loosed in heaven. -Matthew 16:19

Truly, truly, I say to you, whoever believes in me will also do the works that I do; and greater works than these will he do, because I am going to the Father. -John 14:12

Men don't know the power, privilege, and protection we have as God's sons. We have the same power that raised Christ from the dead. This same Holy Spirit lives and dwells among us. We have victory over sin, death, hell, and all darkness. God has filled us with the Holy Spirit. We are Spirit-filled men of God... It's who we are!

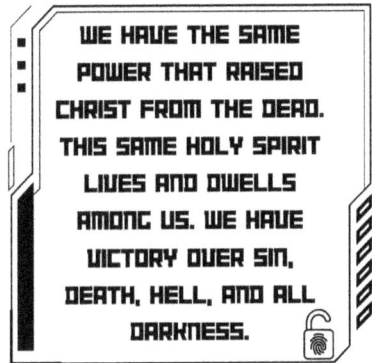

> WE HAVE THE SAME POWER THAT RAISED CHRIST FROM THE DEAD. THIS SAME HOLY SPIRIT LIVES AND DWELLS AMONG US. WE HAVE VICTORY OVER SIN, DEATH, HELL, AND ALL DARKNESS.

2. Our Privilege

I hesitated to use this phrase for this point because, just like the word *identity*, the world is trying to redefine and degrade the word *privilege*. They use the words *"white privilege," "patriarchal privilege,"* etc. as a derogatory term. When I use the word *"privilege"* in this point, I do not mean we have privilege or domination based on our sex or our race. I am referring to the benefits we have as God's sons.

When we confess our sins and ask God to be the Lord and Savior of our lives, we are instantly forgiven and adopted as God's sons. Honest, it's in the Bible!

> *But to all who did receive him, who believed in his name, he gave the right to become children of God, who were born, not of blood nor of the will of the flesh nor of the will of man, but of God. -John 1:12-13*

For all who are led by the Spirit of God are sons of God. For you did not receive the spirit of slavery to fall back into fear, but you have received the Spirit of adoption as sons, by whom we cry, "Abba! Father!" The Spirit himself bears witness with our spirit that we are children of God, and if children, then heirs—heirs of God and fellow heirs with Christ, provided we suffer with him in order that we may also be glorified with him. -Romans 8:14-17

In the same way we also, when we were children, were enslaved to the elementary principles of the world. But when the fullness of time had come, God sent forth his Son, born of woman, born under the law, to redeem those who were under the law, so that we might receive adoption as sons. And because you are sons, God has sent the Spirit of his Son into our hearts, crying, "Abba! Father!" So you are no longer a slave, but a son, and if a son, then an heir through God. -Galatians 4:3-7

See what kind of love the Father has given to us, that we should be called children of God; and so we are. The reason why the world does not know us is that it did not know him. 2 Beloved, we are God's children now -1 John 3:1-2a

We have the privilege and honor of being God's sons. God is our DAD! When we understand this, we can realize our true identity in God. God's sons, it's who we are!

3. Our Protection

I think many struggle with truly knowing their identity as God's sons because we are so heavily bombarded today with ungodly beliefs and opinions. It wears us down. It makes us feel isolated and alone, like we are the only people trying to live for God and obey His Word and commandments.

This constant bombardment makes us feel defeated. It often makes us want to avoid engaging in the fight. It becomes easier to stay quiet, not challenge the cultural norms, and quietly go about doing our own thing. But it is not what we are called to do.

Men of God, we are called to be warriors for God. We are to be the bright light in the dark world, illuminating the evil and corruption with the Biblical truth of God. We aren't called to cower in the corner. We are called to stand!

We are to stand for our families, being a godly model to our children of what it means to serve and follow Christ.

We are to be a voice in the world that seeks to silence us and our beliefs.

We are to be servants in a world that looks to gain power at others' expense.

We are called to extend grace, mercy, and forgiveness in a cruel, unforgiving world, all while standing true to what we believe and know to be right.

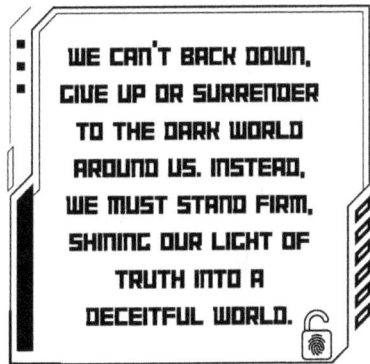

> WE CAN'T BACK DOWN, GIVE UP OR SURRENDER TO THE DARK WORLD AROUND US. INSTEAD, WE MUST STAND FIRM, SHINING OUR LIGHT OF TRUTH INTO A DECEITFUL WORLD.

We can't back down, give up, or surrender to the dark world around us. Instead, we must stand firm, shining our light of truth into a deceitful world.

We can do it because God promised to be our protection.

I have said these things to you, that in me you may have peace. In the world you will have tribulation. But take heart; I have overcome the world. -John 16:33

No weapon that is fashioned against you shall succeed, and you shall refute every tongue that rises against you in judgment. This is the heritage of the servants of the Lord and their vindication from me, declares the Lord. -Isaiah 54:17

Be strong and courageous. Do not fear or be in dread of them, for it is the Lord your God who goes with you. He will not leave you or forsake you. -Deuteronomy 31:6

Fear not, for I am with you; be not dismayed, for I am your God; I will strengthen you, I will help you, I will uphold you with my righteous right hand. -Isaiah 41:10

We have God's hand of protection on our lives. As Psalms 118:6 says, **"The Lord is on my side; I will not fear. What can man do to me?"** A less spiritual way is to throw a little MC Hammer at our fears and say, *"You Can't Touch This...I am a child of God! It's who I am!"*

Throughout the remainder of this book, I want to lay out specific traits of a man of God that make us who we are. Each chapter will serve as both an encouragement and a challenge to help you become a man who knows his true identity as a child of God.

As always, each chapter will have *Group Study Questions* so you can work through them with a group of men. I STRONGLY encourage you to do this. We have been blown away by testimonies of how God has worked through these books as men worked through them together in their men's ministry. There is strength in numbers. Work together with other men. The book also includes a workbook so you can go more in-depth personally, and it can be a format for discussion in your small group.

Are you ready to go? Are you ready to discover your own spiritual identity? Are you prepared to become an unbreakable, unbendable man of God? That's the kind of man God needs in today's world. It's Who We Are. Let's get started.

Group Study Questions:

1. What podcasts do you listen to?

2. Why is it important to know your identity in Christ?

3. How is the world distorting men's identities today?

4. Why is it important to understand the power available to us as God's sons?

5. What does the privilege of being God's son mean to you on a daily basis?

6. How does the idea of God's protection enable us to walk in our true calling?

7. After reading this chapter, what is one thing you will put into practice or one thing you will change in your life?

8. How can we, as a group, help you do this?

CHAPTER TWO
CREATED, NOT EVOLVED

I love superhero movies. Before they started getting into weird, magic, witchcraft-led storylines that my conscience couldn't tolerate, I really enjoyed these movies and stories. Whether it be Tony Stark in a cave, Steve Rogers frozen in ice, or Batman falling in a bat-filled well before the death of his parents, all have compelling origin stories. A beginning, a launching point, something that made them what they were and defined them for all of history.

Everyone has an origin story that helped form who they are. Mankind, in general, even has an origin story. In order to write a book on knowing who you are as a godly man, it is vital that we start in the beginning…all the way in the beginning.

In the beginning, God created the heavens and the earth. The earth was without form and void, and darkness was over the face of the deep. And the Spirit of God was hovering over the face of the waters.

And God said, "Let there be light," and there was light. And God saw that the light was good. And God separated the light from the darkness. God called the light Day, and the darkness he called Night. And there was evening and there was morning, the first day.
-Genesis 1:1-5

Genesis 1 lays out for us exactly how the world, and everything in it, came into existence. God spoke the world into existence. This is an important thing for us all to understand. God created everything. The world did not evolve or come into being by a big explosion or collision. God spoke it into existence by His all-mighty power. This brings us to the first thing we need to look at in this chapter.

1. God created everything, including men.

These verses are so important for us to know and understand. God is the Creator of everything.

Then God said, "Let us make man in our image, after our likeness. And let them have dominion over the fish of the sea and over the birds of the heavens and over the livestock and over all the earth and over every creeping thing that creeps on the earth."

> GOD CREATED MAN IN HIS OWN IMAGE. YOU ARE NOT, HAVE NEVER BEEN, NOR EVER WILL BE A MONKEY OR AN APE. MAN WASN'T AN ACCIDENT!

So God created man in his own image, in the image of God he created him; male and female he created them...And God saw everything that he had made, and behold, it was very good. -Genesis 1:26-27, 31

God created man in His own image. You are not, have never

been, nor ever will be a monkey or an ape. Man wasn't an accident! God, the Maker of the Heavens and the earth, created man. Any other version of Creation is a lie!

After God created Adam, he saw Adam was lonely. God decided to make a woman for Adam so he would have companionship.

> *..for Adam no suitable helper was found. So the Lord God caused the man to fall into a deep sleep; and while he was sleeping, he took one of the man's ribs and then closed up the place with flesh. Then the Lord God made a woman from the rib he had taken out of the man, and he brought her to the man. -Genesis 2:20b-22 (NIV)*

So there we have it. God created Adam out of the dust of the ground in His image, and He created Eve from Adam's rib. The Bible clearly lays out for you the truth of Creation.

Creation isn't just found in Genesis 1. The Bible talks about Creation throughout the entire book. It's in the Old Testament Pentateuch. The Historical Books discuss it. The Poetry Books mention it, and the Prophets reference it. It's in both the Gospels and the Epistles. It is even mentioned throughout the book of Revelations.

Throughout the Bible, we read how we are created by God and in His image. This point is affirmed by the Assemblies of God Position Paper on the Doctrine of Creation:

> *"Both Adam and Eve, male and female, are declared to be made in the "image" and "likeness" of God. These carefully delineated creative acts indicate that humans are distinct from animals. God did not form Adam from some previously existing creature (1 Corinthians 15:39). Any evolutionary theory, including theistic evolution/evolutionary Creationism, that claims all forms of life arose from a common ancestry is thereby ruled out.[1]*

In today's world, secularism is doing everything it can to teach people that Creationism isn't true and that we all evolved from other life forms. They want this to be believed as true and *"the science"* for one specific reason...they hate God. They despise being told they were created in God's image. They do not want any glory going to Him, so they made up the lies of evolution.

We know that the Word of God, the Bible, is absolute truth. It contains no lies. It is the Word of God given to man to guide us through life. Right in the beginning of the Bible, in the very first chapter, it tells us how man was created. That is the end of the argument.

As men, we need to stand for truth. We need to declare that God is the Creator and we are His Creation. If you are a father, it is your job to teach your kids the truth of Creation to counter the lies the school systems are pumping into their heads. I recommend you read the entire *Assemblies of God Position Paper on Creation.* I also recommend reading *Evidence That Demands A Verdict* by Josh McDowell. This timeless apologetics book has information on Creation and Adam as well.

Another great resource is the website *answersinGensesis.com.* Look for other books on Creationism so that you can educate your children and help them learn the truth about Creation.

I was privileged to be able to attend a school that believed in the truth of Creation. They presented the argument of Creationism, as well as evolution. They presented the scientific facts. Have no doubt, there are a LOT of scientific facts and evidence that support Creationism. The other side ignores these scientific facts as they present a slanted, untrue version of Creation. You need to know the scientific facts so you can adequately teach them to your children.

So why is the world denying Creationism and promoting

evolution?

The first reason is because they want to eliminate God from Creation.

The evolutionary side tries to say there was no Intelligent Design, we came to be by accident. But doing this devalues life. They devalue the truth that God created man with a specific plan.

"I have made them for my glory. It was I who created them." -Isaiah 43:7 (NLT)

We were made to bring glory to God. We were made in His image. The secularists, humanists, and evolutionists hate God and don't want to bring Him ANY glory. So they lie about Creation. They lie about the meaning of life. They devalue life. They devalue the soul of man. This devalues the truth of eternity.

We must stand in the gap and speak truth. We were created by God to bring Him glory. He created our bodies, He gave us an eternal soul, and we have a responsibility to love, honor, and serve Him.

> WITHOUT CREATION, THERE IS NO NEED FOR A CROSS.

A second reason the world rejects Creationism is without Creation, there is no Garden of Eden and original sin. No Adam, no apple, no need for reconciliation from sin. If there is no need to be saved, there is no need for a Savior. Thus, they can deny Jesus is the Son of God Who died for the sins of the world. Without Creation, there is no need for a cross.

If we evolved, we can evolve out of our weaknesses. (They use *"weakness"* because no one sins, no one is bad, and everyone is innately good.) Evolution denies our sinful nature, thus we don't need a Savior.

But the truth is God created man and woman with the free choice and free will to follow and serve Him. Adam and Eve disobeyed God, and sin entered the world. Now, all men are born with a sinful nature, and we need a reconciliation with God. This is only possible by the atoning work of Christ at Calvary. He paid our debt and gave us a way back to God! This is a vital point in knowing and understanding who we are!

A final reason the world denies Creation is to promote the LGBTQ agenda. Let's look at the passage in Genesis once again.

> *So God created man in his own image, in the image of God he created him; male and female he created them...And God saw everything that he had made, and behold, it was very good. -Genesis 1:27, 31*

In today's world, this Biblical truth is under attack. The world is pushing a lie that there are more than two genders. For the Bible-believing Christian, there should be no debate. The issue is settled in the verses above.

Genesis 2 provides a more detailed description of how God created man and woman.

> *Then the Lord God said, "It is not good that the man should be alone; I will make him a helper fit for him." Now out of the ground the Lord God had formed every beast of the field and every bird of the heavens and brought them to the man to see what he would call them. And whatever the man called every living creature, that was its name. The man gave names to all livestock and to the birds of the heavens and to every beast of the field. But for Adam[g] there was not found a helper fit for him. So*

the Lord God caused a deep sleep to fall upon the man, and while he slept took one of his ribs and closed up its place with flesh. And the rib that the Lord God had taken from the man he made into a woman and brought her to the man. -Genesis 2:18-22

The Bible is clear. God created a man. The man needed companionship and someone to help him, to balance him, to strengthen his weaknesses. They were created equal, but different, and are two different creations with different skills and abilities. Throughout the Bible, only two genders are recognized: male and female.

Scientifically and historically, whether you are male or female was determined by anatomy and chromosomes.

Ultimately, defining or redefining the definition of *"male"* or *"female"* is not just a societal issue—it is a fundamental attack on Biblical truth and Christianity. Those who believe anything else have fallen under a lie from Satan, seeking to keep people separated from God, from salvation, and God's plan for their lives.

There are not seventy-four genders as many today claim…there are two: men and women. That's what the Bible says, and it's what we must stand firm on as believers.

2. God created you as a man.

It is vital that we understand the fact that God created each of us personally. He designed you personally, yes, you!

For you formed my inward parts; you knitted me together in my mother's womb. I praise you, for I am fearfully and wonderfully made. Wonderful are your works; my soul knows it very well.

My frame was not hidden from you, when I was being

made in secret, intricately woven in the depths of the earth.

Your eyes saw my unformed substance; in your book were written, every one of them, the days that were formed for me, when as yet there was none of them.-Psalms 139:13-16

God created you. He knew you before you were even a gleam in your father's eye. He knew when you would be born. He made you for a purpose. God created all of mankind, but He specifically made you. You are God's handiwork! -Ephesians 2:10

I also want to look at this from a different point of view.

YOU were created as a man. It is who you are. In today's society, there is a huge push to get men to *"transition"* and become women. Notice the push is mainly for men to become women, not so much for women to become men. The world despises men and manhood so much. They hate it so badly that they are encouraging men to mutilate their *"manhood"* and turn themselves into a woman.

But God created you as a man. He created you with the XY chromosome. He created you to be a man and all the responsibility that comes with this. If God wanted you to be a woman, He would have made you with the XX chromosome that a woman has. But He didn't. He made you a man.

The world hates men and manhood so much they are trying to feminize all men. If a man is masculine like he was created to be, they label him toxic.

I despise the term *"toxic masculinity"*. You are not toxic.

Think about that word, *toxic*. The *Merriam-Webster Dictionary* defines toxic as: *poisonous. extremely harsh, malicious, or harmful.*[2]

WebMD defines toxic as: *anyone whose behavior adds negativity and upset to your life.*[3]

GOD DOESN'T MAKE TOXIC MEN!

It is true that men sometimes make bad decisions that lead to sin. But they weren't created to be toxic. No man is created to be an abuser, a liar, or a deceiver. No man is created to degrade women and put them down or abuse them. God didn't design anyone to ever hurt a child. Men, in their sin, make decisions to act toxically, but they weren't created toxic.

God makes leaders. He makes men who understand Biblical servant leadership. He made us to be the strong pillar, the support, the foundation of stability for those in our lives. He created you a man. That is who you are!

GOD DOESN'T MAKE TOXIC MEN!

3. God created your future.

God not only created you in your mom's womb, He created your future. What do I mean? Look at these Bible passages.

> *Before I formed you in the womb I knew you, and before you were born I consecrated you; I appointed you a prophet to the nations. -Jeremiah 1:5*

> *Your eyes saw my unformed substance; in your book were written, every one of them, the days that were formed for me, when as yet there was none of them. -Psalms 139:16*

> *Listen to me, O coastlands, and give attention, you peoples from afar. The Lord called me from the womb, from the body of my mother He named my name. -Isaiah 49:1*

> *But when He who had set me apart before I was born, and who called me by His grace… -Galatians 1:15*

These verses show us such a vital truth we all need to understand. Not only did God create you, **BUT HE CREATED YOU FOR A SPECIFIC REASON, A SPECIFIC PURPOSE!**

Every man reading this chapter was formed and created by God for a specific reason to accomplish a specific goal for His kingdom. Before Jim and Kathy Holden ever thought about being frisky one day, God ordained that I'd be conceived. He planned for me to start and lead Mantour Ministries. Forty-eight years ago, when I was conceived, God already had plans for me to write this very book. That is MIND-BLOWING to me! Yet it is true!

God created you for a specific reason with a specific purpose. Our job as God's men is to find out what that purpose is and do it with every ounce of passion we have!

Your calling may be to be the next Billy Graham. It may be to be a godly father and husband and raise the next Billy Graham. I don't know what you are destined to do for God's kingdom, but I know He has a plan, and it's your responsibility to identify it and do it.

> *Whatever you do, work at it with all your heart, as working for the Lord, not for human masters. -Colossians 3:23 (NIV)*

As a man of God, it is vital to understand that you were created…you did not evolve. You were created for a specific purpose. Your job is to identify this purpose and make it your lifelong goal to do what God created you to do.

Have you discovered your purpose? If not, I encourage you to spend time in prayer and ask the Holy Spirit to reveal to you what God has called you to do for His Kingdom.

Once you discover this purpose, do whatever it takes to fulfill this purpose. Be willing to be educated and learn more. Be open to others teaching you and mentoring you. Use any and all avenues available to you to walk in your calling.

Doing what you were created to do is how you find peace, happiness, and contentment. You were created by the Most High God…it's who you are!

Group Study Questions:

1. Who is your favorite superhero?

2. Why is it essential to believe that God created everything?

3. Why is it important to understand Biblical manhood since society wants to promote gender neutrality?

4. This chapter states, *"God created you for a specific reason with a specific purpose. Our job as God's men is to find out what that purpose is and do it with every ounce of passion we have!"* What does this mean to you?

5. Have you discovered your purpose? How are you walking in this purpose?

6. After reading this chapter, what is one thing you will put into practice or one thing you will change in your life?

7. How can we, as a group, help you do this?

CHAPTER THREE
HEIRS, NOT SLAVES

Recently, I had the pleasure of spending the day with two of my favorite people in the world: a beautiful six-year-old and her adorable four-year-old brother, along with their parents. I love getting to spend time with these kids and playing with them. They bring me such joy. Whether it be a rousing game of *Monkey in the Middle*, them using me as a human sliding board, or telling each other knock-knock jokes and tooting jokes (they call passing gas *"tooting"*), we always have a blast. They are my best buddies!

I spent a day at a lake with them a few months back. They loved throwing rocks into the water, especially big rocks that made a huge splash.

At one point, I sat on the porch watching them and Adessa throwing more rocks into the water. Their dad was sitting next to me, asleep in his chair. All of a sudden, the little girl started screaming bloody murder as her brother went running full speed towards the porch.

I didn't know what had happened! Had a snake bitten her? Did she fall in? Did a thrown rock go off course and hit her in the eye?

Thankfully, it turned out to be nothing that serious. She had a pair of plastic sunglasses, probably from the dollar store, that she was very proud of and had dropped into the lake. This was obviously worthy of all the hysterics!

Her brother ran up to the porch and woke his dad up, telling him what had happened. I watched as they both went to the lake together and saw a father trying to console his unconsolable daughter. Then I saw something that absolutely amazed me.

The young father walked up to the house, went out to his van, and grabbed a pool skimmer. (I do not know why they travel with a pool skimmer, lol. They don't even have a pool!) He walked back to the lake, took off his shoes and socks, and went into the dirty water to get his little princess her $5 plastic sunglasses.

Honestly, I was stunned that he did it. As much as I love this little girl, I wouldn't have gone in after her sunglasses that could have been so easily replaced. But a father's love was different. He saw how badly she was hurting and did whatever he could to fix her pain.

I was also amazed that the father wasn't angry. If I had woken my dad up for something so trivial, he would have exploded that I had lost the glasses and that I had woken him up! But this guy didn't respond in anger at all.

A bit later, Adessa said to the little man, *"You have a good daddy."* He replied to her, *"I think I have a GREAT daddy!"*

He was right. He does have a great daddy. Do you want to know something really interesting about my friend? Growing up, his dad wasn't around. How could he become such a fantastic father without an amazing father of his own? Well, he has an amazing father. He has a Heavenly Father. He is how my friend can be such an amazing, godly man.

Guys, as born-again believers, we are the sons of God. God is our Father. We are heirs of God and His kingdom.

> GUYS, AS BORN-AGAIN BELIEVERS, WE ARE THE SONS OF GOD. GOD IS OUR FATHER. WE ARE HEIRS OF GOD AND HIS KINGDOM.

This is a hard identity truth for so many men to comprehend. There is no nice way to say it other than to say it: We are a fatherless society.

According to the 2022 U.S. Census, approximately 18.3 million children live without a father in the home, comprising about one out of four U.S. children.[1]

This surprisingly high number doesn't account for the number of men who grew up with a father physically residing in the house but nowhere present in their lives, or the men whose fathers abused or mistreated them. Is it any wonder men don't run with open arms to the idea of God as a Father?

To them, seeing God as a Father leads them to see God as someone they can't trust, rely upon, or turn to in time of need. They have guarded walls raised around their hearts, just waiting for God to either abandon them or treat them abusively. It was what they knew about fathers. It's what they expect. So when they are presented with God as their Father, they freak inside.

I understand men like this. I used to feel the same way inside. The last thing I wanted was for God to be my father. To me, that meant controlling, abusive treatment. Having had enough of that in life from my dad, I didn't want anything to do with God being my Father.

Lord, yes. Savior, definitely. But Father? Not on your life!

Then, God began to work on my heart. He showed me that He loves me and only wants what is best for me. I learned from Him that when He is forced to discipline me, it is done out of love and a desire for me to enter into a closer relationship with Him. He is never angry or abusive like my father.

While I still wrestle with realizing that God does love me, I have made progress in changing my image of God and accepting His love as my Heavenly Father. As a result, my actions and behavior have changed as I pursue showing my love for God through living a life obedient to His commandments.

This is what we will look at in this chapter as we look at John 3:1-3. John starts with the assumption that we know God is our Father and then goes on to show what is required of us as His sons.

> *Behold what manner of love the Father has bestowed on us, that we should be called children of God! Therefore the world does not know us, because it did not know Him. Beloved, now we are children of God; and it has not yet been revealed what we shall be, but we know that when He is revealed, we shall be like Him, for we shall see Him as He is. And everyone who has this hope in Him purifies himself, just as He is pure. -1 John 3:1-3 (NKJV)*

John starts off with how great a privilege it is to be God's children. We should have love and gratitude to God for rescuing us from our sins and making us sinless. We should appreciate that He adopted us as His children, with all the rights and privileges of being His children. We are chosen, wanted, and loved.

> *God decided in advance to adopt us into His own family by bringing us to Himself through Jesus Christ. This is what He wanted to do, and it gave Him great pleasure. -Ephesians 1:5 (NLT)*

We have all the rights and privileges that a son has. We are not slaves. We are sons. We have a right to God's inheritance as sons. This inheritance is freedom from sin, eternity in Heaven, and the call to build God's Kingdom here on earth. We aren't slaves to sin or bondage any longer. We are the adopted sons of God.

I am so impressed with people who adopt children. They take hurting, lonely kids and give them a home. Foster parents are also impressive. But there is a difference between being a foster child and an adopted child.

> WE AREN'T SLAVES TO SIN OR BONDAGE ANY LONGER. WE ARE THE ADOPTED SONS OF GOD.

Foster kids are protected and taken care of, and in many cases, treated as the foster parent's own child. But as great as that is, it isn't the same as being adopted.

Adoption gives the adopted child the legal rights and privileges of a naturally born child. Legally, there is no difference than if they were delivered from the mother's body. They have full claim to any inheritance of the parents.

We have this same claim to God's inheritance as His adopted sons. As adopted children, we have the same legal rights as natural-born children.

> *For all who are led by the Spirit of God are sons of God. For you did not receive the spirit of slavery to fall back into fear, but you have received the Spirit of adoption as sons, by whom we cry, "Abba! Father!" The Spirit himself bears witness with our spirit that we are children of God, and if children, then heirs—heirs of God and fellow heirs with Christ, provided we suffer with him in order that we may*

also be glorified with him. -Romans 8:14-27

We have the same rights and privileges as heirs as Jesus. We are co-heirs with Him. God has as much love for us as He has for Jesus.

Jesus is our big brother!

Have you ever had an older sibling? Older siblings naturally look after the younger sibling. They help take care of them. They protect them. And Lord help anyone who comes after a younger sibling. The older sibling will take care of business on their behalf!

Jesus is our big brother. Like a big brother, He has our backs, praying and interceding on our behalf.

This doctrine of sonship as heirs is vital for us to understand and embrace. We are heirs, not slaves. We are members of God's family. As the old Mastercard commercial says, *"Membership has its privileges."* But it also has its responsibilities.

Because we are heirs of God, we should be so grateful that we live a life to please our Father. How do we do this? By living a pure and holy life. This is the mark of a child of God. John continues on to prove this point in verse 5.

> *Whoever commits sin also commits lawlessness, and sin is lawlessness. And you know that He was manifested to take away our sins, and in Him there is no sin. Whoever abides in Him does not sin. Whoever sins has neither seen Him nor known Him*
>
> *Dear children, do not let anyone lead you astray. The one who does what is right is righteous, just as He is righteous. The one who does what is sinful is of the devil, because the devil has been sinning from the beginning. The reason the Son of God appeared was to destroy the devil's work. No one who is born of God will continue to sin, because God's*

seed remains in them; they cannot go on sinning, because they have been born of God. This is how we know who the children of God are and who the children of the devil are: Anyone who does not do what is right is not God's child, nor is anyone who does not love their brother and sister. -1 John 3:4-10 (NKJV)

Someone who loves God and is grateful to Him for saving him and setting him free will express their gratitude by living differently than the world. John says that if we are to abide with God and live with our Father, we cannot also abide in sin. If we are enamored with sin and doing wrong, we are not really serving our Father.

Now, for those of us who have a poor image of a father in our minds, we look at this verse and say, *"See, God is just like my father. He will mistreat me. The first time I step out of line or sin, He will reject me as His son and abandon me."*

However, that is different from what John is saying or even applying. John learned firsthand from Jesus the exact opposite.

And he [Jesus] said, "There was a man who had two sons. And the younger of them said to his father, 'Father, give me the share of property that is coming to me.' And he divided his property between them. Not many days later, the younger son gathered all he had and took a journey into a far country, and there he squandered his property in reckless living. And when he had spent everything, a severe famine arose in that country, and he began to be in need. So he went and hired himself out to one of the citizens of that country, who sent him into his fields to feed pigs. And he was longing to be fed with the pods that the pigs ate, and no one gave him anything.

"But when he came to himself, he said, 'How many of my

father's hired servants have more than enough bread, but I perish here with hunger! I will arise and go to my father, and I will say to him, "Father, I have sinned against Heaven and before you. I am no longer worthy to be called your son. Treat me as one of your hired servants."" And he arose and came to his father. But while he was still a long way off, his father saw him and felt compassion, and ran and embraced him and kissed him. And the son said to him, 'Father, I have sinned against Heaven and before you. I am no longer worthy to be called your son.' But the father said to his servants, 'Bring quickly the best robe, and put it on him, and put a ring on his hand, and shoes on his feet. And bring the fattened calf and kill it, and let us eat and celebrate. For this my son was dead, and is alive again; he was lost, and is found.' And they began to celebrate."
-Luke 15:11-24

While the point of this parable was directed at the Pharisees to show them that they needed to stop being like the older brother and welcome the sinners into the kingdom, this parable beautifully displays how God feels about His sons when they sin.

In this parable of the prodigal son, Jesus taught that it broke the father's heart when his son was enamored with sin and wanted it more than a life with him. The father yearned for his son to realize his sin and return. Daily, he sat watching and waiting for his son to return. He didn't give up on him or abandon him. He wanted him back, and he welcomed him with open arms.

The same is true today. God longs for us to live a pure life before Him. He rewards us with communion and fellowship with Him when we live such a life. When we foolishly reject His love to follow our selfish pursuits, He lets us. However, He never stops loving us and longing for us to return to Him. When we do return, He will welcome us as we begin to change our lives and live as He asks.

This is what it means to be an heir.

As we close this chapter, let's break down this thought of being an heir.

1. God is our Father. He loves us, wants us, and will never abandon us.

God longs for His sons and daughters to return to Him. He wants it so much that He sacrificed His only Son on the cross to provide a way of reconciliation. That was a huge, painful price to pay for you and for me. But He loves us that much!

2. As God's children, we must live a life worthy of being called His sons.

We need to pursue sanctification and become like Jesus. Like a role model, Jesus exemplifies what it means to be God's son. He is our measuring stick and what we should strive daily to be. Each day, we should try to be less like the world around us and more like Jesus.

3. If we are enamored with the world and sin, we are not really God's children. We need to repent and start over with God.

This is such a powerful truth for today's day and age. I see too many in today's church wanting a little bit of God and a lot of the world. But when you are adopted, you don't still live part-time at the orphanage. You live with your new family and adapt to their way of life and customs.

> LEAVE THE ORPHANAGE BEHIND ONCE AND FOR ALL. STOP PURSUING THE WORLD AND ITS EVIL. INSTEAD, LIVE IN YOUR NEW HOME AND FOLLOW GOD AND HIS WAYS.

We need to do the same as God's adopted sons. Leave the

orphanage behind once and for all. Stop pursuing the world and its evil. Instead, live in your new home and follow God and His ways.

4. God will welcome us with open arms as we begin living a life worthy of our calling as His sons.

This is the truth we all need to embrace. We have the unique privilege of being God's children. This is a privilege and an honor. We don't deserve it. Because God has chosen us, we must live in a way that pleases our Father. The good news is that God is there to help us reach our full potential in Him.

One final point that I want to make. When my little friends found themselves in need of help, what did they do? The little guy turned and ran full speed towards his daddy, knowing that he was his source of help.

Guys, when the trials and temptations get to be more than we can bear, we have a Father we can run to for help!

He is always there for us, waiting and willing to help us.

He has a way through the tough times for you.

He gives us the Holy Spirit to comfort us.

He gave us a big brother to intercede for us.

He has all the power and authority available to Him to help us.

He's our father, and we are His boys!

That is who we are, heirs, not slaves.

Group Study Questions:

1. Can you remember a time when you were young when something went wrong, and you had to get an adult to help? Tell this story.

2. How does the truth that God is your father make you feel?

3. This chapter states, *"Someone who loves God and is grateful to Him for saving him and setting him free will express their gratitude by living differently than the world."* How can you personally express this gratitude to God? What steps can you take?

4. Are you doing everything possible to live a life worthy of your calling as heirs? What changes do you need to make?

5. Do you see God as an angry father waiting to punish or a loving father waiting to forgive and welcome you back? What thinking do you need to change?

6. After reading this chapter, what is one thing you will put into practice or one thing you will change in your life?

7. How can we, as a group, help you do this?

CHAPTER FOUR

WARRIORS, NOT WIMPS

I have always been a fan of Superman. What a guy! He was a stranger on a strange planet, endowed with power and strength no one possessed. He could have used this power to conquer and dominate. He could have become a dictator who ruled with an iron fist. But he chose another path.

Instead, he stood for *"truth, justice, and the American way."* He used his power for good, not evil. He never backed down or surrendered. He protected people, helped them, and worked to create peace. Superman was a peaceful, calm man who never wanted a fight. However, he became a mighty warrior and protector when it was necessary. He knew how to balance abusing his power and living in peace with standing up and fighting with everything he had to protect what he believed in.

Men of God, we need to become spiritual supermen. We need to become men who cannot stand by when injustice or evil takes its swing. The world wants all men, especially Christian men, to deny their protective genes deep inside them. They want men to be feminine. They encourage us to stand for nothing and fall for everything. But God calls us to be mighty warriors, not mealy wimps.

God designed men to be protectors. He engrained deep inside us the desire and ability to stand up to injustice, speak out against evil, and stand firm and fight back.

The world hates this masculine trait. They say it is toxic. They call us Neanderthals and brutes. They condemn strong men.

But God loves it when his men are peaceful warriors.

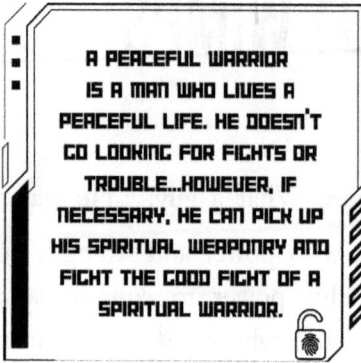

> A PEACEFUL WARRIOR IS A MAN WHO LIVES A PEACEFUL LIFE. HE DOESN'T GO LOOKING FOR FIGHTS OR TROUBLE...HOWEVER, IF NECESSARY, HE CAN PICK UP HIS SPIRITUAL WEAPONRY AND FIGHT THE GOOD FIGHT OF A SPIRITUAL WARRIOR.

Peaceful warrior sounds like an oxymoron, right? Like silent scream, civil war, working vacation, and good female driver (that one will cost me), peaceful warrior doesn't sound like it belongs together because it is the opposite. But it isn't an oxymoron.

A peaceful warrior is a man who lives a peaceful life. He doesn't go looking for fights or trouble. Like Superman, he desires to get along with people to the best of his ability. He isn't mean. He is never abusive. He is a loving man of God. However, if necessary, he can pick up his spiritual weaponry and fight the good fight of a spiritual warrior.

He won't back down or cower under attack. He doesn't turn a blind eye to injustice or danger. He will step in and help those in need. He will destroy evil in his life and work to help others break free. He will defend his family no matter the cost.

This kind of man is a warrior. It is what God has called us to be.

When a man refuses to be a peaceful warrior, it breaks God's heart. Let's look at one of the saddest verses in the Bible to show you what I mean.

> *You are a land that is not cleansed or rained upon in the day of indignation. The conspiracy of her prophets in her midst is like a roaring lion tearing the prey; they have devoured human lives; they have taken treasure and precious things; they have made many widows in her midst.*
>
> *Her priests have done violence to my law and have profaned my holy things.*
>
> *They have made no distinction between the holy and the common, neither have they taught the difference between the unclean and the clean, and they have disregarded my Sabbaths, so that I am profaned among them.*
>
> *Her princes in her midst are like wolves tearing the prey, shedding blood, destroying lives to get dishonest gain.*
>
> *And her prophets have smeared whitewash for them, seeing false visions and divining lies for them, saying, 'Thus says the Lord God,' when the Lord has not spoken.*
>
> *The people of the land have practiced extortion and committed robbery. They have oppressed the poor and needy, and have extorted from the sojourner without justice. -Ezekiel 22:24-29*

I don't know about you, but this sounds familiar to me. It sounds an awful lot like today's world. We have false teachers and progressive Christians spreading false doctrine and lies, tickling people's ears and trapping them in false beliefs and sins. They condone sin and evil and say it is okay.

Our society promotes an evil agenda and sinful ways of life.

Corruption has permeated the highest forms of our government in both parties as they commit crimes and look the other way.

Crime is rising, and some DAs refuse to arrest or prosecute criminals while others are being arrested or canceled for saying or believing things that don't line up with society's agenda. We sound like the nation God looked upon with sadness. Let's continue the passage.

> *And I sought for a man among them who should build up the wall and stand in the breach before me for the land, that I should not destroy it, but I found none.*
> *-Ezekiel 22:30*

How heartbreaking. No mighty warrior was willing to stand in the gap, to stand against all of the evil and fight for God's ways. God just wanted one man, one warrior, who would stand for Him and righteously declare, *"I will not go along, I will not bend, I will not blend, I won't compromise what I believe and know to be true!"*

I believe God is still looking for that today. He is searching for a peaceful warrior who will ignore the world's call to be a wimpy man and instead walk in the strength we have in God.

Guys, we have what it takes to stand in the gap, to be a mighty warrior. We are filled with the Holy Spirit! Just like the sun made Superman invincible, the Holy Spirit strengthens us to fight and win the battle!

> *You, however, are not in the flesh but in the Spirit, if in fact the Spirit of God dwells in you. Anyone who does not have the Spirit of Christ does not belong to him. But if Christ is in you, although the body is dead because of sin, the Spirit is life because of righteousness. If the Spirit of him who raised Jesus from the dead dwells in you, he who raised Christ Jesus from the dead will also give life to your mortal*

bodies through his Spirit who dwells in you.
-Romans 8:9-11

The same Spirit that raised Jesus from the dead is in us! The power that took His dead, lifeless body and breathed life and health back into it breathes inside of us! The supernatural strength that defeated death and hell pulses through our veins. We are equipped to fight!

..no weapon that is fashioned against you shall succeed, and you shall refute every tongue that rises against you in judgment.

This is the heritage of the servants of the Lord and their vindication from me, declares the Lord." -Isaiah 54:17

What then shall we say to these things? If God is for us, who can be against us? -Romans 8:31

We are guaranteed victory. No weapon can defeat us, and no enemy can conquer us. God is for us. Nothing can stand against us. Men of God, it is time to fight!

Who are we supposed to be fighting against?

The Bible is clear about who our enemy is.

Finally, be strong in the Lord and in the strength of his might. Put on the whole armor of God, that you may be able to stand against the schemes of the devil. For we do not wrestle against flesh and blood, but against the rulers, against the authorities, against the cosmic powers over this present darkness, against the spiritual forces of evil in the heavenly places. -Ephesians 6:10-12

We are not fighting against men. We are fighting against Satan and his kingdom. We are fighting against evil and its demonic dark forces. This is important to remember.

It is easy to think we are fighting against people. We can see the progressive Christians as the enemies, or a political ideology we disagree with, or a movement like the LGBTQ+ movement as our enemy. But in reality, the people in these movements have lost their vision of who they are in Christ and who God created them to be. We shouldn't hate them; our hearts should break for them, and we should pray for them to be set free and to find their true hope, Jesus Christ.

> **WE ARE NOT FIGHTING AGAINST MEN. WE ARE FIGHTING AGAINST SATAN AND HIS KINGDOM. WE ARE FIGHTING AGAINST EVIL AND ITS DEMONIC DARK FORCES.**

One of my pet peeves is believers who take to social media and make harsh, cruel posts about homosexuals or transgender people. While I disagree with the sinful lifestyle they choose, as Christians, we must recognize they are trapped and deceived. We fight the wrong enemy when we make cruel and hurtful posts and comments, drawing them further from God instead of bringing them closer to Him.

We need to fight the right enemy. Once we know our enemy, we must fight the good fight of faith. So, what are the battles a warrior fights?

1. We fight to kill sin in our own lives.

Men, before we try and fight for someone else's spiritual freedom, we need to fight for our own.

> *"Do not judge, or you too will be judged. For in the same way you judge others, you will be judged, and with the measure you use, it will be measured to you.*

> *"Why do you look at the speck of sawdust in your brother's eye and pay no attention to the plank in your own eye? How can you say to your brother, 'Let me take the speck out of your eye,' when all the time there is a plank in your own eye? You hypocrite, first take the plank out of your own eye, and then you will see clearly to remove the speck from your brother's eye. -Matthew 7:1-5 (NIV)*

A sick person can't heal another person. All they can do is spread the virus. A doctor with Covid couldn't treat others until he recovered from his sickness. We can't help others break free if we haven't won victory ourselves.

As mighty warriors, we must be brutal to areas of sin in our lives. The Bible never tells us to indulge or entertain sins or wickedness. It tells us to destroy them.

> *Put to death therefore what is earthly in you: sexual immorality, impurity, passion, evil desire, and covetousness, which is idolatry. -Colossians 3:5*

Fight it, destroy it, show it no mercy. Fight the sin and bondages in your life to the death. Like Jacob wrestled with God until God blessed him (Genesis 32:22-32), wrestle with your bondage until you gain victory and freedom.

I can remember times in my life when the Holy Spirit revealed areas of sin in my life. I had to enter the octagon and say to this sin, *"Only one of us is leaving this cage alive!"* I had to fight to gain freedom. I had to confess the sin. I had to remember when it started and what I was doing. I made lists of how it affected me and those around me. I repented to God and anyone else I had sinned against. I developed a battle plan to gain victory and walked out of the cage in freedom, leaving the dead corps of sin inside!

Once I defeated the sin, I developed compassion and mercy for others struggling with the same sin. Because I was a warrior with my sin, I can tell these hurting people, *"I know what you're going through. I've been where you are. I understand your hopelessness. But my God set me free, and He can do the same for you!"*

If I had stayed a wimp, I never could have broken free. But because I became a warrior, I can reach out to other hurting people and offer them a hand in getting out of what traps them.

Guys, you must be a mighty warrior who defeats his sins and struggles. Freedom is there if you will fight!

2. We fight to defend our families.

Guys, we are called to be mighty warriors for our families. Unfortunately, too many men are wimping out and letting the mama bears protect the home.

Guys, we must rise and be mighty men of God in our families. Our calling is to take the spiritual hits in front of our families, protecting them.

We need to be spiritual leaders. We must demonstrate to them how to serve God and walk with Him.

We need to be protecting them in our world. Guys, the world is coming for your kids! They want to instill their worldly ideas and ideology into your children. They don't want you to have a say in what your kids learn or are exposed to at school. They want to advance their sinful agenda by normalizing it in the younger generation. You can see it happening daily.

There are a number of places in this country where the schools bring in drag queens to read to the kids in our schools while normalizing their sinful lives. In some schools and universities, boys become transgender, compete on girls' sports teams, and share a shower and locker room with them. Ten years ago, this would have been sexual assault. Now, it is seen as a right!

You must be involved in your children's education. I personally recommend sending your kids to a Christian school or home school to ensure they are being trained in the way they should go, as we read in Proverbs 22:6. Protect their minds, hearts, and spiritual well-being by removing them from these horrible curriculums and placing them in a godly situation.

If you choose public schools, go to local school board meetings. Run for your local school board and make a difference. A wimp stands by and says, *"There is nothing I can do to change the situation."* A warrior stands up and says, *"Not in my house. I will fight to protect the ones I love".*

3. We fight for Biblical truth.

A wimp goes along with what everyone else says, a mighty warrior stands up for the word of God and defends it.

> **But he said, "Blessed rather are those who hear the word of God and keep it!" -Luke 11:28**

A mighty warrior obeys the Word of God. The world despises the Word. It convicts them of their sin. It shines a light on the evil they believe and practice. They are trying to make the Bible a hate-filled doctrine and say those who believe it are hateful, racist bigots.

But the Word of God isn't hateful. It is God's love in written form. It is God's manual for how to live life. It is designed to convict, transform, and guide.

One of the biggest attackers of God's Word are progressive Christians. Why? Because they don't outright reject it. Instead, they distort it. They intentionally misinterpret it. They water it down and attempt to *"make it relevant"* to today's society and beliefs. They claim to know the truth, and those *"old-fashioned, oppressive"* believers just don't get it.

This is why I speak out so strongly against progressive Christianity. It is so dangerous. Many unbelievers don't know the Bible because they are trapped in sin. Progressive Christians purposely misinterpret the Bible to enjoy their sin and still feel good about themselves. They are leading people to sin and even encouraging it, picking and choosing verses and twisting them to mean what they want them to mean.

Mighty warriors stand on the entire Bible. They believe it and will fight to defend it. It's worth the fight. This brings us to our fourth area to be mighty warriors.

4. We fight against the sinful culture.

We need to stand on Biblical truth, and when the culture goes against God's Word, we need to stand in the gap and say, *"No, this is wrong."*

> **Don't become partners with those who reject God. How can you make a partnership out of right and wrong? That's not partnership; that's war. Is light best friends with dark? Does Christ go strolling with the Devil? Do trust and mistrust hold hands? Who would think of setting up pagan idols in God's holy Temple? But that is exactly what we are, each of us a temple in whom God lives.**
> *-2 Corinthians 6:15-18 (MSG)*

We cannot blend in with the world. We cannot bend to the world's beliefs. We must always avoid temptation and compromise. We must walk a different path. We must fight the good fight of faith and reject the sinful ways of culture.

We must take a stand against injustice. We must reject wickedness and sin. We must fight back against the lies of the culture.

We cannot go along with or live at peace with the world. Wimps excuse sin around them not to make waves. Warriors stand up for what is right and stand firm.

A mighty warrior says, *"We will not bow, we will not bend, we will not "blend in" to keep the peace. Instead, we will stand firm in our faith and refuse to bend and compromise."*

They say, *"No, I can't condone that behavior, that idea, that belief. I can't say that evil is good or wrong is right to avoid conflict. I will not bow to sin, to the culture, to temptation, no matter what. I cannot blend—I must stand for righteousness."*

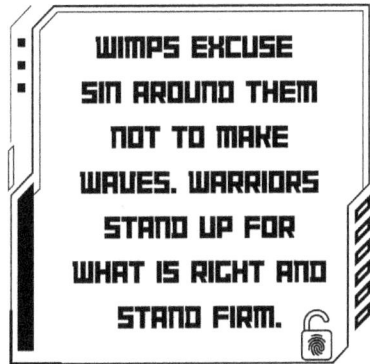

> WIMPS EXCUSE SIN AROUND THEM NOT TO MAKE WAVES. WARRIORS STAND UP FOR WHAT IS RIGHT AND STAND FIRM.

This is a fight worth having. We must stand against the culture and shine bright for God in this dark world.

God has called every one of us to abandon being wimps and instead to be mighty warriors. To stand in the gap. What happens if we refuse to answer this call? Let's look at the end of Ezekiel 22.

> *I sought for a man among them who should build up the wall and stand in the breach before me for the land, that I should not destroy it, but I found none. Therefore I have poured out my indignation upon them. I have consumed them with the fire of my wrath. I have returned their way upon their heads, declares the Lord God."*
> *-Ezekiel 22:30-31*

God had no choice but to destroy Israel and give them over in bondage to their enemies. He found no one standing in the gap to effect change and make a difference. What a sad statement for a nation that was supposed to be God's people.

Guys, the same will happen today if we reject God's call to be mighty warriors. Judgment will fall if no one stands in the gap and fights. We must take this seriously. We must become strong, unmoving, unbending warriors. We must heed Paul's command.

> **Be watchful, stand firm in the faith, act like men, be strong. -1 Corinthians 16:13**

Our identity needs to be men who stand in the gap. It must become part of who we are because it's what we were created to be. So much is riding on us standing in the gap. Will you choose today to be a peaceful warrior and stand for God?

Group Study Questions:

1. Superman had many abilities, i.e., flying, X-ray vision, super strength, etc. What power of Superman do you wish you had?

2. What does it mean to be a *"peaceful warrior"*?

3. Why is it vital for us to remember that we are fighting against evil and demonic dark forces, not our fellow men?

4. What areas of sin have you been entertaining? How can you get brutal with it and destroy it?

5. How does being a peaceful warrior relate to our families?

6. Do you fight for Biblical truth? What are some ways you can do this in life?

7. Do you blend in with culture or bend to pressure? How can you begin to stand in the gap against the evil in society?

8. After reading this chapter, what is one thing you will put into practice or one thing you will change in your life?

9. How can we, as a group, help you do this?

CHAPTER FIVE
LEADERS, NOT RULERS

One of my favorite things is spending time with my friend's little six-year-old daughter and four-year-old son. These two children bring me so much joy! I do nothing but laugh continuously whenever I get to be with them!

I spent the day with them a few months back. At one point, we were playing outside on the deck. The parents didn't want the kids in the house at this point. They wanted them outside, playing and burning off some energy. However, the little guy kept trying to go inside the house. I told him, *"You're supposed to play out here with me. Don't go in the house."*

A few minutes later, Adessa got up and walked off to the house to get a drink of water, and the little boy ran after her like a shot. I didn't think anything of it because he was with Adessa. A few minutes later, he came running up to me with a big smile on his face and proudly proclaimed to me, *"Hey Jamie, you're not the boss. Adessa's the boss."*

Well, his older sister heard what he said and thought it was so funny, so for the next hour, I had two little voices repeating, *"Jamie's not the boss! Adessa's the boss."*

What had happened was this little guy had run up to Adessa to tell her she wasn't allowed in the house either. Adessa asked why couldn't she go in the house, and he replied, *"Jamie said we're not allowed in the house."* Adessa replied, *"Well, Jamie is not my boss."* Thus, the chorus of *"Jamie's not the boss, Adessa's the boss."*

It was funny at the time, but it also was true. I am not my sister's boss. Technically, I am in the structure of the ministry, but I certainly know enough not to lord it over her! She hits hard! (I'm joking! Mostly, lol)

The truth is Adessa and I have learned that the ministry functions and thrives the best when we work together as equals. It would never work if I tried to lead like a dictator. We need each other's abilities and skills.

One of the biggest lies that has permeated Christianity, especially in the 70s and 80s, is that God created men to be authoritarian bosses. Men were the masters, and women and children were to basically bow to their every wish and command. Men were called to ministry, and women needed to stay under a male umbrella. But is this really Biblical?

One of the most significant ways men struggle with being a leader and not a ruler is in the home setting. Much of this is due to poor teaching and doctrine they have received. I know that this was a massive issue in our home growing up.

When I was young, like four or five, my mom and dad started to attend weekend seminars by Bill Gothard, where he taught his *"Basic*

Life Principles." This teaching was doctrinally wrong and taught a lot of oppressive and abusive ways of life. He said his teaching was based on Scripture, but it wasn't. It was based on distorted teaching of the Bible.

Gothard spent an entire weekend teaching his principles of authority and what he called the umbrella principle, which was that everyone had to be under a covering. God was at the top, then the man, the woman, and the kids. He took this idea, twisted it, and distorted it. He taught:

- Men get the best of everything, and everybody else gets the leftovers.

- Men had absolute authority and had to be obeyed regardless of whether it was a sin.

- Children should be physically punished (complete with on-stage demonstrations on how to hit the kids), and kids must be broken. Basically, you had to beat the strong will out of a kid.

- Only men could work. Women were to stay home, raise the kids, and serve their husbands. She couldn't go anywhere or do anything without the approval of her husband. This alienated the woman from other people, so she didn't realize how she was living wasn't normal.

These were just some of the dictatorial, unbiblical teachings taught in these seminars. I won't even get into the sexual teachings and the oppression that brought with it. (If you want to learn more, there is an excellent documentary on Bill Gothard's teachings and all the damage it caused on *Amazon Prime Video* called *"Shiny Happy People."*[1])

My mom and dad would attend these seminars every year and adopted this teaching into our family. It is what I grew up learning. It was literally beaten into me.

It wasn't until I was in my early twenties that I realized this teaching was garbage. When I went to Bible college, I began to see real men of God and how they lived and acted. I saw that what I had been raised in was unbiblical. I had to start unraveling my mind of all this garbage and learn how to be a true servant leader.

Even now, after watching *Shiny, Happy People* on *Amazon Prime,* it revealed areas in our family dynamics that we are working through in our heads and hearts. It has really affected my sister, and she is working hard to remove all of these false teachings from her head.

I tell you all this to show you that I understand the church has had some pretty twisted teachings about manhood and leadership. While the teaching was predominant in the 1970s and 1980s, it is still in the minds of many believers and has seeped into the theology of many churches. As godly men, we must examine our hearts and ensure that our beliefs about leadership and men and women are based on the Bible, not distorted, twisted teaching. We, as men, need to examine the Bible and establish our identity on how God intended us to lead.

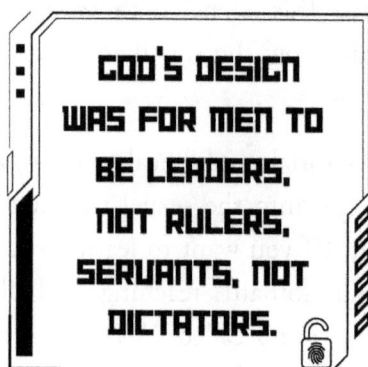

> GOD'S DESIGN WAS FOR MEN TO BE LEADERS, NOT RULERS, SERVANTS, NOT DICTATORS.

I 100% believe God's design was for men to be leaders, not rulers, servants, not dictators.

It isn't always through poor doctrine that we learn this warped view of leadership. Sometimes, it is a cultural thing where a culture teaches male dominance. No matter where we picked it up, we must abandon it, learn Biblical leadership, and become servant leaders.

The simple truth of the matter is this: God never called anyone to be a master. He only calls people to serve. Our job as men of God is to be a servant.

Why does a man need to serve others? The answer is quite simple. We are supposed to follow Jesus's example. Jesus' life was the model of a man who served.

Jesus left the glory of heaven and came to earth to serve others. His entire life was geared toward servanthood. It was the one lesson He constantly drove home to His disciples.

> **GOD NEVER CALLED ANYONE TO BE A MASTER. HE ONLY CALLS PEOPLE TO SERVE. OUR JOB AS MEN OF GOD IS TO BE A SERVANT.**

Within minutes they were bickering over who of them would end up the greatest. But Jesus intervened: "Kings like to throw their weight around and people in authority like to give themselves fancy titles. It's not going to be that way with you. Let the senior among you become like the junior; let the leader act the part of the servant. -Luke 22:24-26 MSG

This is not the only time this happened in the Gospels. It was a real issue for the disciples. Whenever they would go off on another I-am-the-most-important-disciple kick, Jesus gently reminded them they were not called to be masters lording over others. Instead, He called them to serve the least among them. He daily demonstrated this fact to them in how He interacted with them and the people.

The disciples struggled with this teaching because they thought, as Jesus' right-hand men, they deserved to have the least of these serving them. This childish attitude came from a lifetime of the Jewish elite pushing them down and lording over them. Now they were the big wigs, Jesus chosen men, and they were all up for being

the top dog others served.

However, Jesus never let them get away with it. Instead, He taught them what serving means and how to develop a servant's heart. He even demonstrated servanthood when He washed their feet (John 13:1-17).

Many men have fallen into this trap of thinking they get to be a lord over others. But you will not find this anywhere in the Bible. Instead, you will find a call for men to lead with a servant's heart.

Men of God, we cannot continue expecting the precious ones God has blessed us with to serve us. We are to serve them.

Ephesians 5 has some excellent teaching on how a man should treat his family. Let's look at the different relationships.

> *Husbands, love your wives, as Christ loved the church and gave himself up for her, that he might sanctify her, having cleansed her by the washing of water with the word, so that he might present the church to himself in splendor, without spot or wrinkle or any such thing, that she might be holy and without blemish. In the same way husbands should love their wives as their own bodies. He who loves his wife loves himself. -Ephesians 5:25-28*

Ephesians 6 shows how we are to treat our kids.

> *Fathers, do not exasperate your children; instead, bring them up in the training and instruction of the Lord.*
> *- Ephesians 6:4 (NIV)*

These are excellent passages to show how a man should treat others. Paul says a husband needs to love his wife like Jesus loved the church. He needs to lead his children in a loving way that leads them to Christ, not in an abusive manner that turns them off to Christianity and the Bible.

I remember something a counselor told my dad years ago. He was trying to get my father to realize that he needed to forsake the bad teachings he had received and become a servant leader. He said to my dad, "*I bet if I asked you if you would die for your wife, you would say 'yes.' But my question is this: 'Will you live for your wife?'*"

What he was saying is what I am saying in this chapter. A man of God needs to do what Jesus did, lay down his life for others and serve them.

Paul even goes on to show how we are to lead outside of the homes in our jobs.

> **Slaves, obey your earthly masters with respect and fear, and with sincerity of heart, just as you would obey Christ. Obey them not only to win their favor when their eye is on you, but as slaves of Christ, doing the will of God from your heart. Serve wholeheartedly, as if you were serving the Lord, not people, because you know that the Lord will reward each one for whatever good they do, whether they are slave or free.**
>
> **And masters, treat your slaves in the same way. Do not threaten them, since you know that he who is both their Master and yours is in heaven, and there is no favoritism with him. -Ephesians 6:5-9. (NIV)**

Let's start with the essential point that God does not condone slavery as we know it today. The slavery that America experienced before the Civil War was sinful and horrible. It was evil.

In Biblical times and culture, enslaved people were the employees, and masters were the employers. So Paul's teaching should be seen in this light. He is saying a good employee does a good job and gives their bosses an honest day's work, demonstrating godly character while doing it. He also teaches employers to treat their employees well and show them dignity and respect.

Paul teaches us to serve as Jesus served. To understand this passage's full meaning, we must know how Jesus served the church.

When Jesus was on earth, His entire life revolved around serving. If we study the Gospels, we can see ways He served the church that we can apply to our relationships.

He put their needs above His needs. Jesus constantly had thousands of people coming to Him and needing His help and assistance. They had urgent needs and needed His miraculous power to help them. Jesus never turned them away. Even when He was tired or hungry, He put their needs and issues above His needs.

We do this when we look for ways to see others' needs instead of constantly wanting to have our needs met. We serve when we shoulder responsibilities instead of dumping all the responsibilities on others.

Men of God must stop being dictators and realize nothing is beneath them. What do I mean?

A dictator sees something that needs to be done and demands someone else do it. A servant jumps in, meets the need, and gets others to come alongside them.

For instance, I have a mentor who holds a powerful position in the Assemblies of God. Because of this authority, he can tell people to do stuff. He could say, *"Move those chairs over there"* or *"Carry these boxes."* But I haven't seen him do this. I have seen him grab some chairs and move them, and ask someone else to grab a few more chairs or pick up some boxes and ask someone to help with the rest. He leads through service.

Have you ever come home at the end of a long day to find a messy house because your wife was tired after a crazy day of her own?

A dictator would make snide remarks about the mess, making it known he wanted it cleaned up. But would Jesus do that? I don't think He would do this. I think He would start cleaning up the mess. Guys, Jesus washed feet. The least we can do is wash a few dirty dishes.

Another way we show servant leadership is to sacrifice for others. Jesus demonstrated this as well. Jesus' life on earth was filled with service, but His mission was to sacrifice Himself for others. His sole purpose was to lay down His life for all men so they could receive salvation and reconciliation with God.

> JESUS WASHED FEET. THE LEAST WE CAN DO IS WASH A FEW DIRTY DISHES.

A godly leader lives a sacrificial life. He puts the needs of others above his own. He goes without so that the ones he loves have their needs met. I grew up in the opposite. A man's needs were top priority, and everyone else got leftovers. My dad had anything he wanted and got to enjoy any activity or hobby he wanted, no matter the cost, while my mom had one pair of shoes that had to last an entire year. This is the opposite of how it should be.

The Bible says a lot about sacrificing ourselves for others. Here is just a sample.

> *Do nothing from selfish ambition or conceit, but in humility count others more significant than yourselves. Let each of you look not only to his own interests, but also to the interests of others. -Philippians 2:3-4*

> *Greater love has no one than this, that someone lay down his life for his friends. -John 15:13*

By this we know love, that he laid down his life for us, and we ought to lay down our lives for the brothers. -1John 3:16

A real, godly leader sacrifices for others. Their needs and desires take priority. He provides for his kids at his own expense. A godly leader sacrifices his wants, desires, and wishes for others. He lays down his life for others.

Our identity as men of God must require that we are godly leaders. To do this, we must cast off any thoughts or desires of being a dictator or master. We, instead, need to serve and sacrifice for others.

Being a leader and the head of the home means that you are the first one to follow Jesus' example. Seeing your example of Christlike service and sacrifice, your family and employees follow your example.

What do you do if you haven't been living this way but instead have been rolling as a dictator?

Well, the first thing you need to do is ask God to forgive you. Be specific. Allow the Holy Spirit to show you areas where this behavior has infiltrated your life, and repent.

Dive into the Word. Find out exactly what it means to serve like Jesus. Read how He lived and let the Holy Spirit show you where you fall short.

Next, list practical steps you can take to make changes. What can you do differently? What do you need to start doing? What needs to stop?

You must also ask for forgiveness from those you have been treating poorly. Go to them and tell them what you have been realizing and learning, admit you were wrong, and ask them to forgive you.

Finally, move forward, living a sacrificial servant-based life. Don't abandon your calling to lead, but do it with a godly focus, being a servant who sacrifices for others. It's what we are called to do and who we are called to be.

Group Study Questions:

1. What does being *"the boss"* mean to you?

2. This chapter stated, *"God's design was for men to be leaders, not rulers, servants, not dictators."* What does this mean?

3. Do you serve your family or expect to be served?

4. This chapter states, *"Jesus washed feet. The least we can do is wash a few dirty dishes."* What does this mean, and how can you apply it to your family?

5. What steps must you take to change if you struggle with being a dictator instead of a leader?

6. After reading this chapter, what is one thing you will put into practice or one thing you will change in your life?

7. How can we, as a group, help you do this?

CHAPTER SIX
PURE, NOT POLLUTED

2023 has been the weirdest summer ever. All thanks to Canada!

What do I mean? A few weeks ago, I woke up in the morning, and it seemed darker than usual, so I figured it must be raining. But a quick look out the window showed no rain and that the sun was out, sorta.

The sun was in the sky, but you couldn't see it that well. It looked like we were having a very foggy morning, but it wasn't fog. What was it?

It was smoke! Smoke consumed the atmosphere. You could see it, taste it, and smell it. It was horrible.

Apparently, forest fires are burning in Quebec, Canada, over 600 miles away. The smoke from these fires poured into Pennsylvania and the surrounding states, polluting our air quality. New York City had its worst air quality since 9/11. Washington, DC, was covered in smoke. It went as far as Georgia, some 1,400 miles away!

The smoke was everywhere. Being allergic to smoke, I had to stay inside. When I did leave, I had to wear a mask, and it could only be for a short time. If I had chosen to stay outside all day in the smoke-filled air, my throat would begin to close, and I could have eventually died. I couldn't survive in the polluted environment. I needed the pure air found in an air-conditioned home.

Only a fool would choose to endanger themselves like this and say, *"I know the air is polluted. I know it's unsafe. But I am going to go outside anyway."* No one would choose to live in a polluted environment, right?

Wrong. Despite the multiple warnings on the news and social media, people ignored the calls to stay inside and did their own thing. I watched from my front window and saw a guy jogging outside in the air. He ignored the warnings and let his lungs be permeated with the smoke. All across the state, others made similar decisions to ignore sound wisdom and instead pollute themselves in the smoke. People even ended up in the hospital because they ignored the calls to stay inside in unpolluted air.

I don't understand people like that. But they are everywhere. Even Christians make daily choices to allow themselves to be polluted.

Millions of Christian men make this decision daily in their spiritual lives. As men of God, we are called to be pure, not polluted. But instead of pursuing purity in our lives, men are entertaining the pollution around them with dire consequences.

One of my favorite Bible verses is found in Philippians 4:8.

Finally, brothers, whatever is true, whatever is honorable,

whatever is just, whatever is pure, whatever is lovely, whatever is commendable, if there is any excellence, if there is anything worthy of praise, think about these things.

This verse tells us what things we should think about. Notice that one of the words listed is what we are talking about in this chapter... *pure.*

In this Scripture, the word *"Pure"* comes from the Greek word *"hagnos,"* which means *"clean, that is, innocent, modest, perfect---chaste, clean, pure."[1]* It means moral purity of thought and purpose as well as words and deeds.

Barnes defines it as *"Chaste - in thought, in feeling, and in the conversation between the sexes."[2]*

God's will for His men is to be pure. This is especially true when it comes to anything sexual. We cannot call ourselves God's men if we are living a sexually impure life. This not only includes our actions sexually, but it also applies to how we think and the words we say.

The Bible talks quite a bit about the need to be pure.

Draw near to God, and he will draw near to you. Cleanse your hands, you sinners, and purify your hearts, you double-minded. -James 4:8

Who shall ascend the hill of the Lord? And who shall stand in his holy place? He who has clean hands and a pure heart, who does not lift up his soul to what is false and does not swear deceitfully. -Psalm 24:3-4

That last verse from Psalms shows us exactly why it is so important to be pure men. Only the pure can enter God's holy presence! We cannot have a proper relationship with God if we reject purity and embrace sexual impurity.

1 Corinthians 6:9-10 goes even further.

> *...do you not know that the unrighteous will not inherit the kingdom of God? Do not be deceived: neither the sexually immoral, nor idolaters, nor adulterers, nor men who practice homosexuality, nor thieves, nor the greedy, nor drunkards, nor revilers, nor swindlers will inherit the kingdom of God. (NIV)*

WE CANNOT HAVE A PROPER RELATIONSHIP WITH GOD IF WE REJECT PURITY AND EMBRACE SEXUAL IMPURITY.

Christians read this verse and focus on those who practice homosexuality. But notice who else it says won't go to Heaven. It clearly says anyone who is sexually immoral, any adulterer, anyone who is sinning sexually and refusing to change and pursue purity and holiness, is in danger.

This is serious stuff, guys. We must throw off impurity and become men whose identity is purity.

Ephesians 5:3 tells us there shouldn't be a hint of sexual immorality among God's people. No impurity of any kind can be a part of our lives.

Pornography is prohibited.

Sexually explicit TV shows, movies, video games, apps, and music must go.

Sex outside marriage is forbidden, even for divorced or engaged men.

Ephesians 5:4 even says we can't have any coarse jesting or obscene talk. This includes off-colored jokes, double entendres, crude words, or even talk of sex. Godly men shouldn't brag or talk about past sexual sins or past encounters. This all falls under this category.

Guys, we must ensure we are pursuing sexual purity in both words and deeds. Too many men have become too loose with their language. We must speak purely.

Here are some questions to ask yourself:

- Do you change the channel when you see an unmarried couple in bed canoodling together on TV?

- Do you leave a conversation at work or with friends when the coarse jokes or sexual innuendos start flying?

- Do people around you know better than to have off-color conversations around you?

If you said *"NO"* to any of these things, then you are not living the pure life God requires of His men. Even worse, you are in trouble regarding your relationship with God.

We just read in 1 Corinthians 6:9-10 why it is so dangerous. Think about it…if you are looking at pornography when the rapture happens, you could get left behind. God may not take you in the rapture if you are sleeping around. It's not worth the risk. We must become sexually pure men and destroy the idea that men are uncontrollably sexually perverse. The good news is that God is more than willing to help us do it!

I Corinthians 6 says in verse 14 that God has the power to help us. ***"By His power, God raised the Lord from the dead, and He will raise us also." (NIV)***

The same power that raised Jesus from the dead can raise us from sexual death. He has the power to set us free. It takes action on our part.

The first action is a desire to be free. We must want to break free.

We must hate the sexual sins we are committing. God will never take away a sin we want to keep. He doesn't work that way. We must hate the sin and never want it to be part of us again. We cannot use forgiveness as an excuse to keep sinning. We must despise our sexual sin and never want to commit it again.

The second thing we need to do to break free of sexual impurity is to stop blaming others for our sexual sins.

Ok, I am going to get on my soapbox for this one. I am so tired of men of God blaming women for their sexual sins and inability to control their thoughts and minds. It really bugs me.

I hear it all the time, even sometimes preached from the pulpit. *"We are guys. We can't control it. We can't help but notice how they dress. We can't control our thoughts or desires. Women need to do better at not tempting us!"*

This is not only an offensive way to look at women, but it is Biblically untrue! You're telling me the same spirit that raised Christ from the dead can't help you stop sexualizing women?

This form of teaching and belief degrades women. It makes them seem like they are all wiley temptresses trying to seduce every man and steal him away. Number one, get over yourself. They more than likely have zero interest in you.

Secondly, they are daughters of the most high God! God created women to be a helper, to complete man. Face it; man couldn't do the job alone. He needed a woman to help him. She wasn't just a sexual toy. She was a spiritual partner.

Women aren't the problem. Your sexual sin and ways of thinking are the problem. You're degrading women, and looking at them as sexual beings, not spiritual siblings, is the problem. Stop!

Paul told us how to treat and look at women in his words to

Timothy.

> *Do not rebuke an older man but encourage him as you would a father, younger men as brothers, older women as MOTHERS, younger women as SISTERS, in all purity.*
> *-1 Timothy 5:1-2 (emphasis mine)*

Stop blaming women. Realize you have issues. Be willing to face it and take responsibility for it. It's the only way you will live in purity and freedom!

The third step is found in 1 Corinthians 6:18. We must flee sexual immorality.

> *"Flee from sexual immorality. All other sins a person commits are outside the body, but whoever sins sexually, sins against their own body."*

STOP BLAMING WOMEN. REALIZE YOU HAVE ISSUES. BE WILLING TO FACE IT AND TAKE RESPONSIBILITY FOR IT. IT'S THE ONLY WAY YOU WILL LIVE IN PURITY AND FREEDOM!

Sexual immorality is the only sin or temptation we are ever told to run away from. All other sins we are told to stand firm against. However, we must flee from sexual sin.

If the temptation to sin sexually comes from your TV, get rid of it. If you struggle with looking at stuff on the internet, get rid of it. You can live without a PC or a TV, but you cannot live without eternal life and a relationship with God. Get rid of whatever is causing the sin and keeping you from being pure before God.

Pursue accountability. Peer pressure is a great weapon when it comes to fighting pornography. We need men around us who we allow total access to, to ask us any questions, and to hold us accountable whenever they see the need. You need men in your life saying to you:

- What are you watching?

- What are you looking at on your computer?

- What movies and TV are you watching that you know you shouldn't be watching?

- Are you having thoughts about people and women in your life that you shouldn't be having?

These are uncomfortable questions, but we must have this accountability in our lives.

Replace the time spent on devices with Bible reading and prayer. Jesus clearly says that some sins and demonic influences can only be overcome through prayer (Mark 9:29). Remember you are fighting an enemy. Satan and demonic influences are real. Prayer is key to removing their power.

Renew your mind by reading God's Word.

How can a young man keep his way pure? By guarding it according to your word. -Psalm 119:9

It's tough to commit sexual sin at the same time you are reading God's Word. It isn't possible to mix holiness with perversity. Replace the impurity inside with the holy words of God.

Repentance is key to gaining purity. Take King David, for example. David was known as the man after God's own heart. But he allowed himself to drop his guard at one point in his life. Instead of doing what he was supposed to do, leading the army in battle, he decided to stay at home alone and relax.

David gave way to his lust and had an affair with Bathsheba. We are quick to judge Bathsheba in the story, but all she did was take a bath. People say, *"Well, Jamie, she was bathing naked on her roof."*

Are you sure that's in the Bible? Look again at 2 Samuel 11.

> *It happened, late one afternoon, when David arose from his couch and was walking on the roof of the king's house, that he saw from the roof a woman bathing; and the woman was very beautiful. -1 Samuel 11:2*

Notice, nowhere does it say she was a wiley temptress doing a hoochie-coochie dance on her roof. It says David was looking at her FROM HIS ROOF. In reality, all it says is that Bathsheba was taking a bath. Even more, it was a ceremonial bath, an act of worship, purifying herself. (vs 4)

David sinned by lusting after her and degrading her. Nowhere does it say she seduced him. David was the Peeping Tom. It doesn't even say she was a willing party. After all, David was king. Did she even have an option in the matter?

Eventually, David was confronted with his sin, and he was broken. Psalms 51 shows how David repented for his sin with a broken heart.

> *Have mercy on me, O God, according to your unfailing love; according to your great compassion blot out my transgressions.*
>
> *Wash away all my iniquity and cleanse me from my sin.*
>
> *For I know my transgressions, and my sin is always before me.*
>
> *Against you, you only, have I sinned and done what is evil in your sight; so you are right in your verdict and justified when you judge....*
>
> *Cleanse me with hyssop, and I will be clean; wash me, and I*

will be whiter than snow.

Let me hear joy and gladness; let the bones you have crushed rejoice.

Hide your face from my sins and blot out all my iniquity.

Create in me a pure heart, O God, and renew a steadfast spirit within me.

Do not cast me from your presence or take your Holy Spirit from me.

Restore to me the joy of your salvation and grant me a willing spirit, to sustain me. -Psalm 51:1-4, 7-12 (NIV)

David truly repented for his sins. He took responsibility. He didn't blame anyone or anything but himself. King David recognized that he had sinned against God. He realized his impure actions separated him from God and chose to repent.

His beautiful prayer is a model for us to use to repent of our impurity. We can literally pray the same prayer as long as we understand exactly what we are repenting of doing.

Notice what David asked to create inside of him.

Create in me a PURE (emphasis mine) heart, O God, and renew a steadfast spirit within me. -Psalm 51:10 (NIV)

I know this is a prayer God will answer if we pray it with a genuine repentant heart. It's what He wants us to be.

Purity is part of the identity of a man of God. Thankfully, no matter how far you have fallen into sexual pollution and perversity, there is hope and forgiveness. God can and will create a pure heart inside of you. All He needs is a repentant, willing heart who wants to change and live differently. A man who will sacrifice whatever he needs to sacrifice and do whatever he needs to do to break free.

I gave you clear steps you can take to embrace purity. These steps are crucial to living a pure life. When people see you do these things and live a morally and sexually pure life, they will know you are different.

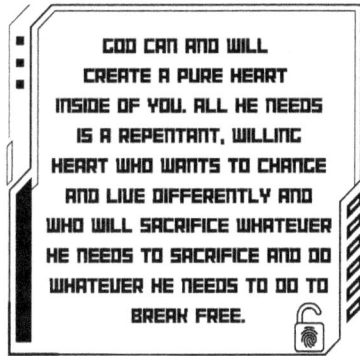

> GOD CAN AND WILL CREATE A PURE HEART INSIDE OF YOU. ALL HE NEEDS IS A REPENTANT, WILLING HEART WHO WANTS TO CHANGE AND LIVE DIFFERENTLY AND WHO WILL SACRIFICE WHATEVER HE NEEDS TO SACRIFICE AND DO WHATEVER HE NEEDS TO DO TO BREAK FREE.

Honestly, the world expects Christians to be different in this area. When you overcome, they will see the difference in your life, and you will have broken the bad reputation. When all Christian men work together to break free from their sexual sins and live a godly, moral lifestyle, we can start a new reputation for men that God's men live a pure life. Then we can say, *"Pure, it's who we are."*

Group Study Questions:

1. Is there anything you're allergic to, like smoke?

2. This chapter states, *"We cannot have a proper relationship with God if we reject purity and embrace sexual impurity."* Why is this true?

3. Do you change the channel when you see an unmarried couple in bed canoodling together on TV?

4. Do you leave a conversation at work or with friends when the coarse jokes or sexual innuendos start flying?

5. Do people around you know better than to have off-color conversations around you?

6. Have you been guilty of blaming women for your sexual issues? If so, have you repented?

7. Do you have an accountability partner? If not, will you commit to finding one?

8. After reading this chapter, what is one thing you will put into practice or one thing you will change in your life?

9. How can we, as a group, help you do this?

CHAPTER SEVEN
FOLLOWERS, NOT FANS

I love Christmas movies! Whether it be a modern classic like *Elf* (which was released almost 20 years ago) or an old-fashioned classic like *It's A Wonderful Life*, I am on board for a good Christmas flick!

One of my family favorites is Irving Berlin's *White Christmas*. What a great movie! We watch it every season. However, I don't think anyone watches it the way I do.

You see, I fast-forward through most of the singing and dancing. I'm sure I just ticked off many people with that revelation. I know, it is a musical, but it drives me crazy how it just goes on and on.

However, among all the singing and dancing that seems to go on forever, there is one song I really like and listen to every time, *The Old Man.*[1]

This song is actually sung twice in the movie. It's the song the soldiers sing in appreciation to their commanding officer, Major General Thomas Waverly, who is about to retire. It's a great song about how they'd follow the General anywhere. Why are they so loyal? The answer is in the song…because they love him.

This song demonstrates the loyalty soldiers feel to their commanding officers. It is also an excellent metaphor for how we, as God's men, should feel about following and serving God. We should follow God wholeheartedly because we love Him and are so grateful to Him for all He has done for us.

Like the soldiers in the movie, we should be willing to follow God anywhere and do anything for Him, to sacrifice anything and everything for Him. That's being a faithful follower.

Unfortunately, too many would-be followers today turn out to only be fans of Jesus. What do I mean?

Well, let me show you by examining how Jesus encountered the same thing in His day and age.

Let's look at John 6. For the sake of space, I'm going to summarize the background of this passage before we look at the meat of the chapter I want us to focus on. You can read the whole chapter yourself to make sure I'm accurate.

In John 5, Jesus and His disciples entered Jerusalem to celebrate one of the Jewish festivals. While there, Jesus healed a lame man at the pool of Bethesda, only to be challenged by the religious leaders for healing on the Sabbath and for saying God was His Father. After His verbal sparring and takedown of the religious leaders, Jesus, and His disciples went to the other side of the Sea of Galilee.

John 6 tells us that a massive crowd who had seen His stunning miracles followed Him across the sea. Jesus taught the people and performed one of His most infamous miracles, feeding 5,000 people with four small loaves of bread and two fish.

This miracle only made Jesus more famous, and His crowds grew larger.

That night, Jesus' disciples crossed the Sea of Galilee in a boat to reach Capernaum, and Jesus stayed behind. The disciples got caught in a horrible storm, and we see Jesus perform two more amazing miracles here. He calmed the storm, but even more impressive, He walked across the lake on the water!

This miracle spread His fame even more. The people rushed to Capernaum to be with their new hero, Jesus. It looked like Jesus' big day had finally come. He had so many people following Him! However, Jesus understood something. Some of the people were true followers, but not everyone. What do I mean? Let's pick it up in verse 22.

> *On the next day the crowd that remained on the other side of the sea saw that there had been only one boat there, and that Jesus had not entered the boat with his disciples, but that his disciples had gone away alone. Other boats from Tiberias came near the place where they had eaten the bread after the Lord had given thanks. So when the crowd saw that Jesus was not there, nor his disciples, they themselves got into the boats and went to Capernaum, seeking Jesus.*
>
> *When they found him on the other side of the sea, they said to him, "Rabbi, when did you come here?"*
>
> *Jesus answered them, "Truly, truly, I say to you, you are seeking me, not because you saw signs, but because you ate your fill of the loaves. -John 6:22-26*

Jesus knew they weren't genuinely following Him for the right reasons. They didn't want salvation and forgiveness of sins. They wanted free food and for Jesus to do miracles. They weren't there for spiritual reasons. They wanted dinner and a show!

Jesus understood this. It would have been easy for Jesus to revel in His fame and crowd size. But He knew His mission, to seek and save the lost. He decided to give them some tougher teaching to separate the fans from the true followers.

> *Do not work for the food that perishes, but for the food that endures to eternal life, which the Son of Man will give to you. For on him God the Father has set his seal." Then they said to him, "What must we do, to be doing the works of God?" Jesus answered them, "This is the work of God, that you believe in him whom he has sent." So they said to him, "Then what sign do you do, that we may see and believe you? What work do you perform? Our fathers ate the manna in the wilderness; as it is written, 'He gave them bread from heaven to eat.'" -John 6:27-31*

Jesus gave them some real spiritual meat to digest, and their response was, *"Let's get back to the dinner and a show. Give us miracles and food, and we'll believe You."*

Once again, Jesus tries to redirect them to a spiritual discussion.

> *Jesus then said to them, "Truly, truly, I say to you, it was not Moses who gave you the bread from Heaven, but my Father gives you the true bread from Heaven. For the bread of God is he who comes down from Heaven and gives life to the world." They said to him, "Sir, give us this bread always." -John 6:32-34*

Jesus is talking about faith and salvation from sins. The people are stuck on wanting a free meal and entertainment. They want to be fans of Jesus because of what they get from Him. But they aren't hungry for HIM, His words, His life-giving message. They want more tuna sandwiches!

Jesus knew they didn't really want to follow Him. But He is always willing to receive anyone who is, so He decides to give them the straightforward, honest truth about why He is really there.

> *Jesus said to them, "I am the bread of life; whoever comes to me shall not hunger, and whoever believes in me shall never thirst. But I said to you that you have seen me and yet do not believe. All that the Father gives me will come to me, and whoever comes to me I will never cast out. For I have come down from Heaven, not to do my own will but the will of him who sent me. And this is the will of him who sent me, that I should lose nothing of all that he has given me, but raise it up on the last day. For this is the will of my Father, that everyone who looks on the Son and believes in him should have eternal life, and I will raise him up on the last day." -John 6:35-40*

This is one of the first times Jesus really lays out His true purpose in ministry. He came from Heaven to save men from their sins. He was their way, their truth, and their life, the way to be reconciled to God and receive eternal life.

A true follower would have recognized this truth and rejoiced. They would have dedicated their lives to following Jesus because of their gratitude for salvation. But that's not what happens.

> *So the Jews grumbled about him, because he said, "I am the bread that came down from heaven." They said, "Is not this Jesus, the son of Joseph, whose father and mother we know? How does he now say, 'I have come down from heaven'?" -John 6:41-42*

They didn't repent. They got offended. How dare Jesus speak to them like this?!? After all, this was just Joseph and Mary's kid. They knew Him His whole life! How dare He say He's from Heaven with the answers they need?

Undeterred, Jesus goes even deeper to separate the followers from the fans.

> *Jesus answered them, "Do not grumble among yourselves. No one can come to me unless the Father who sent me draws him. And I will raise him up on the last day. It is written in the Prophets, 'And they will all be taught by God.' Everyone who has heard and learned from the Father comes to me— not that anyone has seen the Father except he who is from God; he has seen the Father. Truly, truly, I say to you, whoever believes has eternal life. I am the bread of life. Your fathers ate the manna in the wilderness, and they died. This is the bread that comes down from Heaven, so that one may eat of it and not die. I am the living bread that came down from Heaven. If anyone eats of this bread, he will live forever. And the bread that I will give for the life of the world is my flesh." -John 6:43-51*

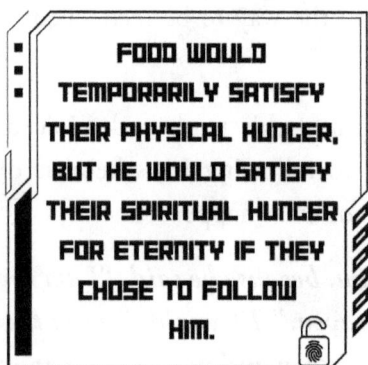

FOOD WOULD TEMPORARILY SATISFY THEIR PHYSICAL HUNGER, BUT HE WOULD SATISFY THEIR SPIRITUAL HUNGER FOR ETERNITY IF THEY CHOSE TO FOLLOW HIM.

Jesus really went for the truth here. He straight out told them, *"I am the Bread of Life. I give salvation. I restore you to God."*

This is the first of the seven *"I Am"* statements Jesus makes in the Gospels. Each *"I Am"* revealed a vital part of His mission. This *"I Am"* shows us that Jesus is our source of spiritual nourishment. He is the answer to our spiritual hunger deep inside. Food would temporarily satisfy their physical hunger, but He would satisfy their spiritual hunger for eternity if they chose to follow Him.

These words of Jesus missed their mark with the multitude of fans. Jesus gave them great spiritual truth, but what did they hear?

> *The Jews then disputed among themselves, saying, "How can this man give us his flesh to eat?" -John 6:52*

Talk about missing the point! Jesus is offering them salvation and freedom from sin, and they are trying to figure out if He is really offering to let them take a bite out of Him! Seriously?!?

Jesus continued on, unfazed.

> *So Jesus said to them, "Truly, truly, I say to you, unless you eat the flesh of the Son of Man and drink his blood, you have no life in you. Whoever feeds on my flesh and drinks my blood has eternal life, and I will raise him up on the last day. For my flesh is true food, and my blood is true drink. Whoever feeds on my flesh and drinks my blood abides in me, and I in him. As the living Father sent me, and I live because of the Father, so whoever feeds on me, he also will live because of me. This is the bread that came down from Heaven, not like the bread the fathers ate, and died. Whoever feeds on this bread will live forever." -John 6:53-58*

Jesus is making it clearer than He ever had before. He was their only way to receive eternal life. They had to choose to follow and obey or reject and leave. Jesus wanted true disciples, not fans with selfish motivations.   What was the final response?

> *When many of his disciples heard it, they said, "This is a hard saying; who can listen to it?"... After this many of his disciples turned back and no longer walked with him. -John 6:60, 66*

The fans had reached their breaking point. Jesus wasn't giving them what they wanted. They were seeking freebies, entertainment, and miracles. Jesus was offering a relationship and a way of life. This isn't what they wanted, so they turned and walked away.

How sad! Yet it happens to this day!

So many would-be followers of Jesus are fans following God for what they will get out of it. They want blessings, health, posterity, and happiness. They don't want a Lord having authority over their life, a Savior showing them areas of sin, or a Restorer sanctifying them daily. They want the good stuff, the fun stuff. They are fans of God, not faithful followers.

Jesus always gives us a choice: to follow or not to follow. That's exactly how this passage ends.

> **So Jesus said to the twelve, "Do you want to go away as well?" Simon Peter answered him, "Lord, to whom shall we go? You have the words of eternal life, and we have believed, and have come to know, that you are the Holy One of God." -John 6:67-68**

> **A FOLLOWER FOLLOWS THROUGH THICK AND THIN, GOOD AND BAD, ROUGH AND TOUGH. THEY STAY LOYAL.**

My man! I love Peter. What a follower! He wasn't perfect by any means, but he was devoted and committed to following Jesus, no matter the cost!

That is a true follower. A follower follows through thick and thin, good and bad, rough and tough. They stay loyal.

Fans, on the other hand, don't. Our world today is full of fans. The entire progressive Christian movement is a movement of fans.

Fans want to feel good about themselves for being religious. They want all the good parts of religion. But they also don't want to make any waves, make anyone too uncomfortable, or go through anything too tough.

Fans are fickle, while true followers are faithful.

Fans want to hang onto the sins they enjoy. They want the ooey-gooeys of Christianity without the hard following part.

Following God entails a deeper level of commitment, belief, and personal relationship compared to being a fan. It involves actively seeking and aligning one's life with the Bible and everything it teaches. Fans pick and choose what they accept and reject from the Bible.

Following God requires a personal and ongoing commitment, while being a fan may involve a more casual or superficial engagement.

A follower is willing to become more like Jesus in every area of life, while a fan of Jesus simply admires or respects His message. But if that message challenges them too much, they walk away.

Fans are in it for what they can get, and if the costs outweigh the rewards, they bale. Followers, on the other hand, embrace the good times and the bad, choosing that no matter what, they will pick up their cross and follow Jesus.

God is looking for a generation of men to rise up and be true followers. Our identity should be totally and completely devoted to God, developing a relationship with Him, and becoming more Christ-like daily. God doesn't want any more fans. He wants sold-out believers. Fans break His heart because He knows they are missing out on what He truly has for them.

Here's a big difference between being a follower and a fan. Fans don't want God or the Bible to cramp their style or keep them from doing what they want. They like Jesus, but they also like the world and the world's ways.

Guys, we need to decide every day to be a follower, deny ourselves and our desires, go wherever God wants us to go, or do whatever He wants us to do. Followers understand there is no highway option in God's Kingdom. They don't embrace the *"my way or the highway"* attitude. They instead choose to walk on the straight and narrow path.

I don't know about you, but I want to be a true-blue follower of Jesus. I want my identity to be a man who is committed wholeheartedly to God no matter what. I want the same for you. I've made my choice. Now it's your turn. Will you follow Jesus?

Group Study Questions:

1. What's your favorite Christmas movie?

2. What's the difference between a follower and a fan?

3. Have you ever been guilty of being more of a fan of God than a follower?

4. What steps can you take to move from fandom to following?

5. This chapter states: *"We need to decide every day to be a follower, deny ourselves and our desires, go wherever God wants us to go, or do whatever He wants us to do."* What are practical ways of doing this?

6. After reading this chapter, what is one thing you will put into practice or one thing you will change in your life?

7. How can we, as a group, help you do this?

CHAPTER EIGHT
VICTORS, NOT VICTIMS

What did you want to be when you grew up? I'm sure we all had visions of what we would be as an adult when we were a child. Some of my dreams for adulthood were to be the Lone Ranger (I was a kid; I didn't know this wasn't possible), a third baseman for the Philadelphia Phillies, a quarterback like John Elway, a chiropractor, and the list goes on. It all really depended on what I was into at the time.

I am not different from most of you. I am sure you had heroes that you dreamed of one day emulating. Each of us had dreams of what we wanted our lives to be.

No matter what you secretly hoped for your future, I bet that not one of us grew up dreaming of becoming a victim one day. No one aspires to this. However, victims seem to be the norm of the day.

IT'S WHO WE ARE

EVERYONE is a victim in today's society. It's almost become the hip new trend. Everyone has an oppressor. Everyone has been trampled down by someone. Too many are embracing this identity. Christians are even embracing it.

I am here to tell you today…YOU ARE NOT A VICTIM! You are a victorious son of the most High God! It's who you are!

That's why we are going to discuss in this chapter the need to reject all victimhood in our lives.

What exactly does the word victim mean?

Webster's Dictionary defines a victim as *one that is acted on and usually adversely affected by a force or agent. One that is subjected to oppression, hardship, or mistreatment.*[1]

This is such a vital chapter if we are to identify our true identity as godly men. This chapter is burning inside of me. I am so sick of the victim mentality in today's world, I could literally puke!

People embracing victimization has been growing exponentially. Every day, we run across someone in life or on social media who makes it clear that they're always living in a victim mentality. Some people think they're victims of their parent's behavior. Other people are victims of abuse or poverty or society. Many feel they have been victimized in their church or by other Christians. The entire deconstruction movement of progressive Christianity is built on being a victim of the church. People who constantly embrace a victim mentality make it difficult for others who really have been victims of things in their lives and are genuinely trying to heal.

Often, people embrace being a victim because they don't want to take responsibility for actions they have taken in life, decisions they have made, or things that they've done wrong in life.

Too many people are walking around, embracing their

victimhood instead of standing up and gaining victory. The sad thing is that many people claiming victimhood are victimizers.

What do I mean?

Male athletes claim to be women and compete in women's sports, dominating the events and taking away victories and success from women who have trained their whole lives. But today, the women fighting back against it are the victimizers, and the male athletes are the victims.

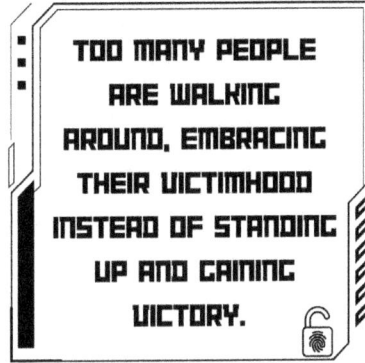

> TOO MANY PEOPLE ARE WALKING AROUND, EMBRACING THEIR VICTIMHOOD INSTEAD OF STANDING UP AND GAINING VICTORY.

People are stealing from stores all across America. If an employee tries to stop them, the employee gets fired, and the thief gets away. Why? Because the criminals are just victims of society and need the things they steal.

I could go on and on. Everyone today wants to be a victim. It has become a brand, an identity. People are victims of racism, sexism, ageism, patriarchy…the list is never-ending.

It is heartbreaking to watch and even more heartbreaking to see men of God adopt this attitude. No man of God has the right to claim they are a victim! Why? Because there is no sin, bondage, weakness, struggle, stronghold, or oppression that the power of God cannot help you overcome. We are not victims. We are filled with the power of the Holy Spirit. We are victorious!

God calls us to throw off a victim mentality. It has no place in the life of a believer. Victimhood is the state of powerlessness, but we are filled with the power of the Holy Spirit! This power allows us to gain victory and rise above anything we face in life.

> **VICTIMHOOD IS THE STATE OF POWERLESSNESS, BUT WE ARE FILLED WITH THE POWER OF THE HOLY SPIRIT!**

The Apostle Paul knew and exhibited this to us. Paul was a man who victimized many people before he was saved. He went around persecuting and killing believers out of a sense of duty to his God. Thankfully, he had a life-changing conversion and became the amazing man of God we know today.

Paul's life was anything but easy, though. Let's look at some of the things on the checklist of Paul's life that he endured.

• Went to jail as an innocent man ☑

• Lashed ☑ ☑ ☑ ☑ ☑

• Beaten ☑

• Faced death—countless times ☑

• Flogged ☑

• Beaten by rods ☑ ☑ ☑

• Stoned with rocks ☑

• Shipwrecked ☑ ☑ ☑

• Lost in the open sea ☑

• Forged rivers ☑

- Fought off thieves ✅

- Betrayed by friends ✅

- Forced labor ✅

- Went hungry ✅

- Sleep deprivation ✅

- Nakedness ✅

- Loss of possessions ✅

(2 Corinthians 11:23-33)

If you continue into chapter 12, you read that Paul had a huge physical disability that hindered him, and he would beg God repeatedly to take it away from him. But God refused to remove the physical problem from Paul. So Paul was disabled, beaten, jailed, constantly on the run, facing trials and persecutions left and right. If there was anyone in the Bible who should have adopted a victim's mindset and identity, it was Paul!

But that is never Paul's attitude. Paul didn't use words like *pity, victim, defeated, overwhelmed,* etc. He used words like *stand firm, press on,* and *move forward.* Paul's attitude was always to face whatever he had to face, go wherever God sent him, endure whatever pain he faced, press through any difficult circumstances, and stand firm against any attacks of the enemy he encountered. Defeat was never an option for Paul. Instead, his attitude was that he would do whatever it took to gain victory. Check out the words of this remarkable man of God.

> *But thanks be to God, who gives us the victory through our Lord Jesus Christ. -1 Corinthians 15:57*

> *Now thanks be to God who always leads us in triumph in Christ, and through us diffuses the fragrance of His knowledge in every place. -2 Corinthians 2:14 (NKJV)*

> *What then shall we say to these things? If God is for us, who can be against us? -Romans 8:31*

> *I know how to be brought low, and I know how to abound. In any and every circumstance, I have learned the secret of facing plenty and hunger, abundance and need. I can do all things through him who strengthens me. -Philippians 4:12-13*

Here is my favorite of Paul's words of victory:

> *We are afflicted in every way, but not crushed; perplexed, but not driven to despair; persecuted, but not forsaken; struck down, but not destroyed; -2 Corinthians 4:8-9*

I love those verses. I originally planned on this entire chapter being based on that verse in 2 Corinthians alone, but God had other plans. But what words of victory!

> **PAUL NEVER EMBRACED A VICTIM'S ATTITUDE. HE EMBRACED VICTORY IN CHRIST!**

Do you read even a hint of victimhood in Paul's words? I sure don't! His affliction didn't crush him. His perplexity and bewilderment never turn into despair. Despite his constant persecution, he always saw God's hand of protection! He got knocked down, but he got up again! You couldn't keep him down or destroy him!

In these verses, I see the words of a man who lives victorious through the power of the Holy Spirit! He never embraced a victim's attitude. He embraced victory in Christ!

"But Jamie, I'm not the Apostle Paul, and you don't understand what I'm facing in life."

You're right. I don't know what you're facing. But God does, and He has precisely what you need to gain victory.

I don't mean to sound trite. I understand what it's like to face hardships and how easy it is to embrace a victim's attitude. Really, I do.

I struggle daily with a physical disability. I have a neurological disease that causes my limbs to be crippled, especially my right foot. It also affects my hands. It is a progressive, degenerative disease, meaning the older I get, the worse it will get. I struggle daily with simple tasks most take for granted, such as standing in a shower or buttoning a pair of pants. If you see me wearing a lot of workout pants instead of jeans, that's why. I can't button pants anymore. Someone has to do it for me.

Last October, I developed a tumor on my big toe. It was the most painful thing I had ever faced in my life. It hurt SO BAD! They removed it surgically, but I couldn't put any weight on my foot for over a month. During this month, my foot turned severely. Instead of walking on the right side of the bottom of my foot, it turned so severely that I literally walk on the side of my foot. (At least the bottoms don't get callouses anymore.) I can now barely walk at all.

Let me tell you, I have had to fight to the death the desire to become a victim, to roll over and say, *"I give up."* The struggle has been real! But I have fought this victim state of mind! I am not a victim. I am a victor!

I have found ways to adapt to this new physical situation. I started using a knee scooter to get around. It keeps me mobile and the rest of my body active and moving. I have begun kneeling on a chair with one leg while standing on my other leg when I cook a meal. I just ordered a collapsable stool to stand when I preach, one foot on the ground and one knee on the stool. I am facing new and challenging situations, but instead of embracing victimhood, I have embraced solutions that allow me to continue walking in God's calling on my life until such a time as God chooses to heal me.

Recently, at a Mantour Conference, a man came up to me after my message and said, *"You know what I appreciate about you? You are such an amazing example of overcoming physical struggles. When I see you, I don't see your disability. I see your joy. It ministers to so many who are facing difficult situations."*

I will always remember these words. I wear them like a badge of honor, not because of anything great about me, but because it is a testimony to the power of God. If that man only knew the daily battle to reject victimhood and embrace victory! It's a constant battle! But to sample a little from Paul, *"Thank you, God, for giving me the victory!"*

Guys, this can be your testimony, too! You do not have to spend your whole life as a victim. Man up and embrace the victory that is promised to you through Christ!

How do you do it? Honestly, the first step you need to take is to answer this question: *Do you really want to stop being a victim?*

Sounds easy. Of course you do! But do you really? It is so easy to say the words, but continue on the path of finding your identity in your victimhood. You have to honestly decide if you want to be free.

Next, you need to become a warrior and fight the attitude of victimhood. Throw it off. Repent to God for allowing this attitude to develop and grow in your life. Spend time in prayer, working with God to resolve your grief, anger, resentment, and roots of bitterness. Then, begin replacing the victim mentality with a Biblical, godly state of mind.

Then dive into God's Word like never before! Let the words of the Bible renew and regenerate your mind. Allow the Holy Spirit to transform your outlook and thought process. Reject all forms of self-pity, negativity, and victimhood.

Finally, allow the power of the Holy Spirit to move inside of you and lead you to victory. Whenever a victim or defeatist attitude tries to gain ground again, instantly throw it down and reject it. Give it zero oxygen in your life!

> JUST BECAUSE SOMEONE KNOCKS YOU DOWN DOESN'T MEAN YOU HAVE TO STAY DOWN! IT'S TIME TO GET BACK UP!

But Jamie, I have been victimized by other people. You don't know how bad it's been and what's been done to me. How do I overcome this real-life victimization?

I get this. Sometimes, people really are the victims of other people's actions. I personally was a victim of abuse. It is real. It happened. But it doesn't have to define you! Just because someone knocks you down doesn't mean you have to stay down! It's time to get back up!

If you are a man who is struggling to gain victory, you may need to seek help from a Christian counselor to help you work through the things and the relationships that caused you to be a victim. I have done this myself, it is worth the time, effort, and cost.

No man of God is created to be a victim. You were created and designed to live a victorious life with God. It's your identity… It's who you are and who you must be!

Group Study Questions:

1. When you were a kid, what did you want to be when you grew up?

2. What does it mean to be a victim?

3. Have you struggled with feeling like a victim? In what ways?

4. This chapter states, *"A victim mentality...has no place in the life of a believer. Victimhood is the state of powerlessness, but we are filled with the power of the Holy Spirit!"* What does this mean practically?

5. Do you want to stop being a victim? No matter the cost?

6. How does reading the Bible help us overcome being a victim?

7. After reading this chapter, what is one thing you will put into practice or one thing you will change in your life?

8. How can we, as a group, help you do this?

CHAPTER NINE
DOERS, NOT HEARERS

As I said earlier in this book, I spend a lot of time in my car driving and listening to podcasts. The other day, I was listening to one of my favorite sports talk shows[1], and they talked about an interesting dilemma in the life of one of the hosts.

Apparently, he had driven his car through wet paint. A truck in front of him had a giant bucket of paint fall off the back, and he didn't see the ensuing paint puddle and went straight through it.

The paint splattered everywhere. It covered the wheel wells. It splashed onto the side of the car and all across the back. It was a huge mess.

Instead of dealing with the mess, the car owner just stewed about it but didn't clean it up. He let it sit on the car…for days. Each day, they would give updates on the lack of progress on his car.

The other guys on the show told him what to do to get rid of the paint. They told him how to clean it and even offered to help him. A professional car detailer even called into the show and provided words of wisdom. He told him exactly what cleaner to use and how to remove it. He also told him, *"Do not take your car through a car wash. The car wash chemicals will seal the paint in and make it even harder to get the paint off".*

The car owner was a truly blessed guy. He had friends offering to help him clean the car. He had professionals telling him precisely what to do. So, what was his course of action?

He ignored everything they said to him. He didn't let them help him clean it. He didn't use the cleanser that they recommended. Instead, he did the one thing everyone told him not to do. He ran his car through a car wash!

As a result, he had to take it to a professional body shop and pay hundreds of dollars to remove the paint. All because he refused to listen and do what he was told. He listened to what they said; he just chose to ignore it and not do it.

I do not get this attitude. I do not understand why someone would shun advice designed to help them in a tough time. Why not listen to someone who wants to help you and do what's best for you? Why avoid words of wisdom that are for your own good?

It happens every day, though. People reject advice and help. They listen to what people say, and then they do the opposite. It even happens in churches and Christian homes.

What do I mean?

Daily, believers ignore the commands of God in the Bible. The Bible is filled with the words of God Himself. God, in His love and wanting what is best for us, gave us a book, a blueprint, for how we as believers should live our lives. Yet, daily, believers read God's Word but don't practice it.

They go to church, but don't put into practice what they hear. They listen to podcasts but don't make any changes. They watch Christian reels on social media and hit the like button without actually contemplating what they could apply.

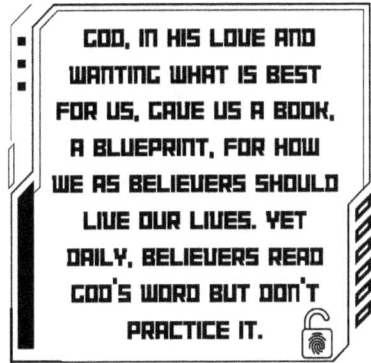

> GOD, IN HIS LOVE AND WANTING WHAT IS BEST FOR US, GAVE US A BOOK, A BLUEPRINT, FOR HOW WE AS BELIEVERS SHOULD LIVE OUR LIVES. YET DAILY, BELIEVERS READ GOD'S WORD BUT DON'T PRACTICE IT.

We have so much information available to us, yet many listen to it but don't actually do it. They are hearers of the Word, but not doers.

It is no wonder James tells us in the first chapter of his book:

> **But be doers of the word, and not hearers only, deceiving yourselves. -James 1:22**

The *Fire Bible* gives excellent insight into this verse. It says:

> *"We deceive ourselves when we think that being exposed to Bible teaching and Christian ministry is enough to keep us in the right relationship with God. We can be involved in all kinds of church activity and ministry and know a lot about God's Word; but if you're not putting that word into practice, all of our activity and knowledge is meaningless. You must develop true godly character and a lifestyle based upon our companionship with Christ in order to truly please God, fulfill His purposes for our lives, and receive ultimate spiritual salvation."*[2]

We are called to be doers, not hearers. Our calling is to let the Word of God change us, make us into new, sanctified believers, and grow into spiritual warriors.

How does reading the Bible help us do this? James continues:

..if anyone is a hearer of the word and not a doer, he is like a man who looks intently at his natural face in a mirror. For he looks at himself and goes away and at once forgets what he was like. But the one who looks into the perfect law, the law of liberty, and perseveres, being no hearer who forgets but a doer who acts, he will be blessed in his doing. -James 1:23-25

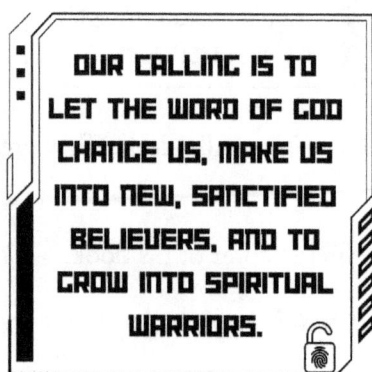

> **OUR CALLING IS TO LET THE WORD OF GOD CHANGE US, MAKE US INTO NEW, SANCTIFIED BELIEVERS, AND TO GROW INTO SPIRITUAL WARRIORS.**

Personally, I wouldn't say I like looking into mirrors very much. It exposes that I am getting older. I see the white hairs on my head. For most of my life, I've never been able to grow a beard, and now that I can, it grew in gray and white! I see some wrinkles and the formation of a double chin. The mirror exposes my true appearance and flaws. The worst is a hotel mirror with fluorescent lighting; it shows every flaw! Unlike a selfie on our phones, there is no filter to make us look like we want to look in a mirror. It just reflects what's really there.

The Word of God exposes what is inside of us. It helps us see areas of sin we are still struggling with in our lives. The Holy Spirit convicts us as we read the Word, and this conviction should lead us to make changes if we are genuinely doers and not just hearers. If we don't make the changes the Holy Spirit shows us, we won't retain what the Bible says. We will forget it, and it won't be available to us the next time we are in a quick draw gunfight with the enemy. (Sorry, some of last year's cowboy theme is still inside of my head, lol)

James isn't the only man in the Bible who teaches us to read God's Word and then do what it says.

Jesus said in John 14:15-16:

If you love me, show it by doing what I've told you. I will talk to the Father, and he'll provide you another Friend so that you will always have someone with you. (MSG)

Paul tells us in Romans 12:2:

Do not be conformed to this world, but be transformed by the renewal of your mind, that by testing you may discern what is the will of God, what is good and acceptable and perfect.

How do we renew our minds? By reading God's Word. Seeing how few Christians even take this first step breaks my heart. Just look at this stat.

Between early 2019 and 2020, the percentage of US adults who say they use the Bible daily dropped from 14% to 9%, according to *the State of the Bible 2020 report* released by the Barna Group and the American Bible Society. Only 14% of people said they read God's Word daily, pre-pandemic. That is so sad! But it has been even worse since the Covid-19 pandemic. Now, only 9% read God's Word daily.

The numbers are equally pathetic for believers. *A Lifeway Research* survey in 2019 found that only 32% of Protestant Christians read the Bible daily. 27% read it a few times a week. 12% once a week, and 5% once a month. 12% of Protestant Christians say they never read God's Word![3]

How are we supposed to do what the Bible tells us if we aren't even reading the Bible?!? Guys, this is not how it should be. We must become men who daily read the Bible.

It's easy for us to say, *"I am so busy. God understands if I don't read the Bible every day. I go to church and hear the messages, at least."*

Okay, first, you need to read the Bible. But let's go with this line of reasoning. You go to church and hear the message.

Do you take notes?

How often do you respond at the altar?

How often do you make practical changes based on what you heard preached?

Are the sermons changing you, or are you just listening to them?

Okay, now let's blow this argument out of the water. Going to church is not enough to sustain you spiritually. Think about it. How long is the average sermon?

Well, the *Pew Research Center* actually did a study on this and found that the average sermon is 37 minutes long.

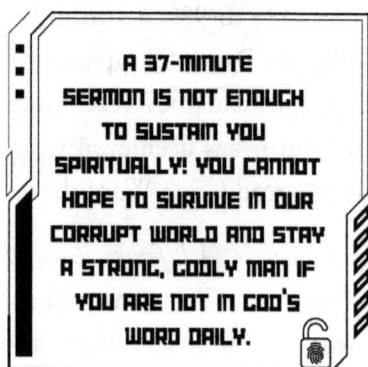

> A 37-MINUTE SERMON IS NOT ENOUGH TO SUSTAIN YOU SPIRITUALLY! YOU CANNOT HOPE TO SURVIVE IN OUR CORRUPT WORLD AND STAY A STRONG, GODLY MAN IF YOU ARE NOT IN GOD'S WORD DAILY.

"Catholic sermons were the shortest, at a median of only 14 minutes, compared with 25 minutes for those in mainline Protestant congregations and 39 minutes in evangelical Protestant congregations.

Meanwhile, historically black Protestant churches had by far the longest sermons — at a median of 54 minutes."[4]

Let's go with the average of a 37-minute sermon. One week is 10,080 minutes. So, for 37 minutes a week, you receive godly influence in your life. For the other 10,043 minutes a week, you are being influenced by the world. Even if you take the highest number of 54 minutes, that is still 10,026 minutes of worldly influence.

That is not enough to sustain you spiritually! You cannot hope to survive in our corrupt world and stay a strong, godly man if you are not in God's Word daily.   You will live a defeated, unfulfilled life. And worse, you will not become the man God created you to be.

No wonder Jesus gave us a fantastic metaphor about what happens when we do not act upon what we read and hear in the Word.

> *"Everyone then who hears these words of mine and does them will be like a wise man who built his house on the rock. And the rain fell, and the floods came, and the winds blew and beat on that house, but it did not fall, because it had been founded on the rock.*
>
> *And everyone who hears these words of mine and does not do them will be like a foolish man who built his house on the sand. And the rain fell, and the floods came, and the winds blew and beat against that house, and it fell, and great was the fall of it." -Matthew 7:24-27*

A foundation is so crucial to the security of a home. I recently watched a show on HGTV where a sub-contractor was supposed to reinforce a foundation for an existing house. He poured the new and improved foundation for the house but didn't use any rebar.

When the homeowner and the general contractor found this out, they were furious. Why? Because they had to rip out all the work the subcontractor did and redo it using rebar. Even worse, the access point for the cement truck was gone, and they had to wheelbarrow all the cement into the foundation.

It cost thousands of dollars because the subcontractor didn't produce a solid foundation. Still, they all knew that if it wasn't done correctly with rebar, the three-story house would fall down and be destroyed.

Guys, how strong is your foundation?

Is your life built on hearing AND OBEYING the Word of God? If the answer is *no,* you will fall when the trials and temptations of life rage against you. Those aren't my words. They are Jesus' words!

The man who chooses to reject the truth of God's Word is placing his life on sinking, shifting sands that will not stand up when the storms of life come. The man of God who chooses to read the Word of God, understand what it says, and obey God's Word is building his life on a solid foundation.

Like a solid, firm foundation, the man who builds his life on the Word of God will always be secure.

Do you want your life to have a secure foundation?

Then, you need to become a man of the Word.

You need to read it, study it, and choose to build your life around it by applying it to your life. You need to be a doer!

So how can you practically become a man who is a hearer, not a doer? Here are some ideas:

• Take notes during a church sermon.

• Respond at the altar call.

• After church, think of one thing you need to do differently this week.

• Sign up for the *It's What We Do Mantour Ministries Daily Bible Reading Plan* via email, or purchase the paperback version. Daily read the passage and allow the Holy Spirit to show you areas to change.

• Be quick to respond to conviction from the Holy Spirit. Don't just brush it off. Repent, make changes, and apply what the Bible says.

- Daily, tell your spouse or a friend what you read in the Bible and what changes you need to make. Accountability helps.

- Just do it. Daily read the Bible.

Guys, these are just a few practical steps you can take to ensure that you are a man with a solid foundation built on the rock. They are ways to go beyond just hearing God's Word to actually doing what it says. Don't continue to go through life with paint splattered all over you. Take spiritual action to clean up your mess because that is our true calling, to be a doer, not just a hearer. It's who we are!

Group Study Questions:

1. Have you ever spilled paint on a valuable surface? What did you do to fix the mess?

2. Do you spend time daily in God's Word?

3. This chapter states, *"Our calling is to let the Word of God change us, make us into new, sanctified believers, and grow into spiritual warriors."* How can you begin to do this?

4. Do you take notes in church?

5. How often do you consciously decide to make a change after hearing a sermon?

6. Is your life built on hearing AND OBEYING the Word of God?

7. After reading this chapter, what is one thing you will put into practice or one thing you will change in your life?

8. How can we, as a group, help you do this?

CHAPTER TEN
COACHES, NOT COMPETITORS

Recently, I listened to a sports show discussing comments made by Steelers' legendary quarterback Ben Roethlisberger.

Big Ben, as he's affectionately known by Steelers loyalists (of which I am not one, Go Broncos!), was speaking about how, in the 2022 season, he was actively rooting against the Steelers' new rookie quarterback that had replaced him after he retired. He talked about how he hoped Kenny Pickett would struggle and fail because he felt he still had something left in the tank and didn't like that somebody had replaced him and forced him into retirement.

As I heard these comments, I cringed inside. What a horrible attitude for a veteran football player to have, especially one who is a professed born-again Christian. Honestly, I was embarrassed for Big Ben. I don't think he realized how petty he sounded.

Big Ben had lost his identity as a football star. Instead of being a good teammate and wanting what was best for the team, he focused on his stature, reputation, and fame. Instead of offering up the wisdom and expertise that he had accumulated and learned over the years in the league to help Kenny Pickett be a better quarterback and leader, he went so far as to cheer and rejoice in his mistakes and shortcomings. He was hoping Kenny would fail.

Big Ben made a mistake I see so many men of God make in their lives. Instead of knowing who they are in God and being secure in this knowledge, they look to advance themselves more and more. Instead of following the Bible's commands to make disciples and teach them the ways of God, they get intimidated by younger people who could outdo or replace them.

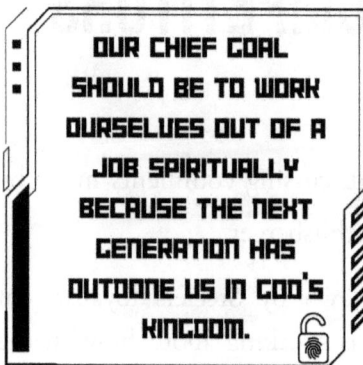

> OUR CHIEF GOAL SHOULD BE TO WORK OURSELVES OUT OF A JOB SPIRITUALLY BECAUSE THE NEXT GENERATION HAS OUTDONE US IN GOD'S KINGDOM.

Men, we need to be raising up the next generation of godly men. It is our mission and responsibility to demonstrate to them what it means to live and act as a man of God and be willing to let them outgrow us and outdo us in God's kingdom.

One of my favorite quotes ties into this topic.

"My generation's ceiling is the next generation's floor."

I love this quote. This should be the definition of mentorship. This motto is the attitude all men of God should adopt. We should encourage the next generation to surpass us spiritually! We should never discourage them to promote ourselves and our interests. A real man of God hopes the next generation goes above and beyond what he is doing and then does all he can to help them do it!!!

God called us to be spiritual coaches, not competitors! Our chief goal should be to work ourselves out of a job spiritually because the next generation has outdone us in God's Kingdom. There will come a point where we go from being the spiritual quarterback to being the spiritual cheerleader, cheering on the new leader and offering our wisdom and encouragement.

Let me show you an example of this in the Bible. We will look at 2 Samuel 7:1-3 at one of the OG men of God who knew who he was and what he needed to do to grow God's Kingdom.

> *Now when the king lived in his house and the Lord had given him rest from all his surrounding enemies, the king said to Nathan the prophet, "See now, I dwell in a house of cedar, but the ark of God dwells in a tent." And Nathan said to the king, "Go, do all that is in your heart, for the Lord is with you."*

David, grateful to God for all He had done to bless His life, wants to show his gratitude by building a grand temple to God. The prophet blessed the project, but unfortunately, neither David nor Nathan checked in with God before filing for the building permit.

> *But that same night the word of the Lord came to Nathan, "Go and tell my servant David, 'Thus says the Lord: Would you build me a house to dwell in? I have not lived in a house since the day I brought up the people of Israel from Egypt to this day, but I have been moving about in a tent for my dwelling....*
>
> *When your days are fulfilled and you lie down with your fathers, I will raise up your offspring after you, who shall come from your body, and I will establish his kingdom. He shall build a house for my name, and I will establish the throne of his kingdom forever. I will be to him a father, and he shall be to me a son. When he commits iniquity, I will*

discipline him with the rod of men, with the stripes of the sons of men, but my steadfast love will not depart from him, as I took it from Saul, whom I put away from before you. And your house and your kingdom shall be made sure forever before me. Your throne shall be established forever.'" -2 Samuel 7:4-6, 12-16

God tells David that he was not to build a temple for Him. It was not God's will or timing. However, God says that in the future, He will allow another man, a younger man, a successor, one of David's sons, to build Him a temple.

Now, David has a decision to make here. He can either accept what God says and go with it, realizing his ceiling in life has been set by God and do what he can to help the next king soar above and beyond him, or he can pout and sulk because he will be outdone and surpassed by another. What decision did David make?

Let's look at 1 Chronicles 22. As we do, we will see lessons we can learn to help us help younger men surpass us in God's Kingdom as we become coaches, not competitors.

1. David Set Solomon Up To Succeed

Then David said, "Here shall be the house of the Lord God and here the altar of burnt offering for Israel."

David commanded to gather together the resident aliens who were in the land of Israel, and he set stonecutters to prepare dressed stones for building the house of God. David also provided great quantities of iron for nails for the doors of the gates and for clamps, as well as bronze in quantities beyond weighing, and cedar timbers without number, for the Sidonians and Tyrians brought great quantities of cedar to David. For David said, "Solomon my son is young and inexperienced, and the house that is to be built for the

Lord must be exceedingly magnificent, of fame and glory throughout all lands. I will therefore make preparation for it." So David provided materials in great quantity before his death. -1 Chronicles 22:1-5

David didn't pout about God's decision. He didn't rebel and disobey God. He didn't try to undermine Solomon or make it harder to protect his legacy. He did the opposite. He realized his son was young and inexperienced, so he did everything he could to make the project easier for Solomon.

God told him he couldn't build the temple, but He never said he couldn't plan it, stockpile for it, and gather a reliable workforce to ensure Solomon succeeded. David realized an important point we all need to learn: The work is about God's Kingdom, not personal accomplishment. Who cares who gets the credit as long as the job gets done and God's kingdom grows?

Men, it isn't about us. It's about God's kingdom. No matter how hard you may try to outdo someone else in ministry, if it is God's will for them to outdo you, you won't be able to stop it. So get out of their way, get behind them, and do what you can to advance God's will. It's who we are!

2. David Taught Solomon How To Succeed

1 Chronicles 28:9-20 says:

"And you, Solomon my son, know the God of your father and serve him with a whole heart and with a willing mind, for the Lord searches all hearts and understands every plan and thought. If you seek him, he will be found by you, but if you forsake him, he will cast you off forever. Be careful now, for the Lord has chosen you to build a house for the sanctuary; be strong and do it."

Then David gave Solomon his son the plan of the vestibule of the temple, and of its houses, its treasuries, its upper rooms, and its inner chambers, and of the room for the mercy seat; and the plan of all that he had in mind for the courts of the house of the Lord, all the surrounding chambers, the treasuries of the house of God, and the treasuries for dedicated gifts; for the divisions of the priests and of the Levites, and all the work of the service in the house of the Lord; for all the vessels for the service in the house of the Lord, the weight of gold for all golden vessels for each service, the weight of silver vessels for each service, the weight of the golden lampstands and their lamps, the weight of gold for each lampstand and its lamps, the weight of silver for a lampstand and its lamps, according to the use of each lampstand in the service, the weight of gold for each table for the showbread, the silver for the silver tables, and pure gold for the forks, the basins and the cups; for the golden bowls and the weight of each; for the silver bowls and the weight of each; for the altar of incense made of refined gold, and its weight; also his plan for the golden chariot of the cherubim that spread their wings and covered the ark of the covenant of the Lord. "All this he made clear to me in writing from the hand of the Lord, all the work to be done according to the plan."

David laid it all out for Solomon. He told him about God's command for his life and Solomon's life. He showed him the plan he had made but was unable to carry out. Then he showed him the outlines, blueprints, and tools and supplies he had prepared. He basically gave Solomon a *"Build a Temple"* kit. All he had to do was assemble it. Solomon was set to succeed, and David taught him how to do it.

A man with David's attitude is hard to find. We far more often find Big Ben's, not King David's. Whether it be an out-and-out defiance or a tamer, more passive/aggressive feeling of *"I learned a lot doing it the hard way, I wouldn't want to deprive them of this experience,"* men leave the next generation high and dry to ensure they don't get outdone.

My brothers, this is not who we are as men of God! We should be doing anything and everything we can to help them succeed.

I have a friend who models this to me all the time. He has a position of authority in ministry, but he understands that he is only one man and can only do so much. Instead of holding back other men like me, he lets us loose to minister, coaches us as we go, and teaches us what we need to do to succeed. He realizes it is about more than him...it is about advancing the kingdom. As long as that gets done, he will let others do it.

Guys, such a man is a gem and, unfortunately, hard to find. However, it is the type of man we all need to develop into.

3. David Gathered Others To Help Solomon Succeed

> *David also commanded all the leaders of Israel to help Solomon his son, saying, "Is not the Lord your God with you? And has he not given you peace on every side? For he has delivered the inhabitants of the land into my hand, and the land is subdued before the Lord and his people. Now set your mind and heart to seek the Lord your God. Arise and build the sanctuary of the Lord God, so that the ark of the covenant of the Lord and the holy vessels of God may be brought into a house built for the name of the Lord." -1 Chronicles 22:17-19*

David could have been content to teach Solomon and then take full credit for Solomon's success; after all, he taught him everything he knew! But that wasn't David's heart. His heart was to make his ceiling Solomon's floor, to have Solomon outdo him and surpass him. So he gathered strong, capable men around Solomon and told them, *"You work for him now, do everything you can to make him shine!"*

The friend I mentioned earlier did the same for me. When we started planning our conferences ten years ago, he not only allowed me to take charge of them and plan them, he not only helped me pick speakers, but he also went to the speakers and told them to work with me and make sure the conferences succeeded. Following David's example, he ensured I received help from many sources, not just him. He sets an example we can all follow.

It can be such a dangerous temptation to want to be the sole voice and influence to a younger man, especially if we see potential in them. It is a temptation to want to ride their successes and say, *"They got where they are or did what they do because of me."* Ok, you probably wouldn't say it out loud, but it would be a thought in your head that you would find a less self-aggrandizing way to say it publicly so that others got the message.

But this attitude will stunt their spiritual and leadership growth. They won't reach their full potential with just one point of view or one person's guidance. Like it or not, no matter how amazing a man of God you are or how much growth and change you have accomplished, you will not be wholly sanctified until you get to heaven. You still have blind spots in your life or issues you struggle with. They need more than your input.

I have been blessed with amazing men of God who have poured into my life, but I also know that these men are not perfect, nor are they right 100% of the time. Other points of view are invaluable to be able to bob and weave through the challenges in life.

Very few teams have just one coach who handles it all. Take

football, for example. There is a head coach of the team, but there are also assistant coaches and coordinators who excel in specific areas of expertise. The head coach encourages his players to learn from these coaches and grow better as athletes. The same principle applies here. Be secure enough to let others speak into your mentees' life. It will only be for their good and growth.

4. David Prayed For Solomon To Succeed

> *O Lord our God, all this abundance that we have provided for building you a house for your holy name comes from your hand and is all your own. I know, my God, that you test the heart and have pleasure in uprightness. In the uprightness of my heart I have freely offered all these things, and now I have seen your people, who are present here, offering freely and joyously to you.*
>
> *O Lord, the God of Abraham, Isaac, and Israel, our fathers, keep forever such purposes and thoughts in the hearts of your people, and direct their hearts toward you. Grant to Solomon my son a whole heart that he may keep your commandments, your testimonies, and your statutes, performing all, and that he may build the palace for which I have made provision." -1 Chronicles 29:16 -19*

David made sure to pray for Solomon's success. He understood that no matter how much he prepared for Solomon to succeed, no matter how much he taught Solomon to succeed, and no matter how many people he surrounded Solomon with to help him succeed, he could never succeed without God's blessing. So David held Solomon up in prayer and asked God to help him accomplish what God called him to do.

I think too often we, as men, don't realize the true power of prayer. I cannot tell you how often my mom would try (with little success) to get me to change my actions and behaviors, but in my rebellion, I wouldn't submit and obey. Instead of giving up on me, my mom hit her knees and prayed for me. And her prayers were not wasted. God heard her prayers and honored them. I have changed in so many areas of life and become the man she saw I had the potential to be, and I believe her prayers had a massive part in it.

Pray for your younger mentees. Pray for a powerful, fresh anointing on their lives. Pray for them to change areas that need to be changed. Pray for their success. Ask God to make them into the mighty men of God you know they are destined to be. We are to be mighty men of prayer. It's who we are!

Guys, David was a fantastic man in his own right and had an incredible legacy. He was Israel's greatest king. His epitaph for all history is *"A Man After God's Own Heart."* Every king in Israel's history after David was compared to David as to whether he was a success or failure. But even with this legacy, David had to step aside and let the younger men take over. He had to understand that his job was to let his floor in life be their ceiling, and he had to do all he could to make them soar. If someone as amazing as David had to do this, why would we ever think we wouldn't?

> A REAL MAN OF GOD REALIZES HIS TRUE CALLING IN LIFE IS NOT TO BUILD KINGDOMS BUT TO TRAIN KINGS!

A real man of God realizes his true calling in life is not to build kingdoms but to train kings! We don't need to rack up accomplishments; we need to rack up successors who can go out due us. We achieve our most significant success in God's kingdom when we take off our helmets and become cheerleaders. We MUST become coaches, not competitors. When we realize this, God's kingdom will be unstoppable. So I encourage you to adopt this motto for life:

"My generation's ceiling is the next generation's floor."

Become a coach, not a competitor. It's a massive part of who we are!

Group Study Questions:

1. Who is your favorite quarterback of all time?

2. What are some ways you can help your younger teammates succeed?

3. What is one lesson you can teach a younger man to help him succeed in God's kingdom?

4. What prayers can you pray for a younger man?

5. What does this phrase mean to you: *"A real man of God realizes his true calling in life is not to build kingdoms; it is to train kings!"*

6. After reading this chapter, what is one thing you will put into practice or one thing you will change in your life?

7. How can we, as a group, help you do this?

CHAPTER ELEVEN
INFLUENCERS, NOT INFLUENCED

The other day, I read something that shocked me. According to a CBS News article, 86% of kids today want to grow up to become social media influencers.[1] I know what you are probably thinking. *"Just what we need, more precocious YouTubers pretending to be celebrities telling us everything we do wrong."*

I may resemble that thought. It was my initial reaction. But to today's kids, being an influencer is our day's desire to play third base for the Phillies or be the lead singer in a rock band. To them, it is celebrity, power, and prestige.

In this chapter, I want us to look at the need for all of God's sons to adopt the identity of an influencer. I don't mean being an influencer as a noun like kids today do. We need to use it as a verb, something we do, actions we take.

The Bible is filled with commands from God for us to make a difference in the kingdom. Let's examine a few.

1. We are to be salt in a tasteless world.

In His most famous sermon, Jesus taught us that we need to be what is most people's favorite seasoning, salt.

> *You are the salt of the earth. But if the salt loses its saltiness, how can it be made salty again? It is no longer good for anything, except to be thrown out and trampled underfoot. -Matthew 5:13 (NIV)*

> **AS MEN OF GOD, WE NEED TO COMMIT TO GETTING SALTY.**

The *Fire Bible* study notes on this passage give a great explanation for what it means to be salt.

Salt seasons and flavors food just as a Christian should enhance and favorably influence the people and society around them. Salt is a preservative, just as a Christian and the church should resist moral corruption and decay, preserving a godly influence on the culture. Salt has healing properties, just as Christ followers must help bring healing to people who are hurting physically, emotionally, and spiritually. Salt also creates thirst, just as Christians, through their good examples, should create spiritual thirst or desire in others to know more about God.[2]

God calls us to influence the world the way salt influences everything it touches. French fries are so much more desirable with salt than without it. A foot bath with salt is more soothing and healing than soaking your feet in plain old water. Salt preserves meat so it doesn't spoil or go bad. Salty popcorn drives us to grab a Pepsi to quench the thirst it creates.

As spiritual salt shakers, we help drive people away from sin and evil and toward God and His kingdom. As men of God, we need to commit to getting salty.

2. We are to be light to a dark world.

The very next thought in Jesus' Sermon on the Mount is another call to influence the world around us.

> *You are the light of the world. A town built on a hill cannot be hidden. Neither do people light a lamp and put it under a bowl. Instead they put it on its stand, and it gives light to everyone in the house. In the same way, let your light shine before others, that they may see your good deeds and glorify your Father in Heaven. -Matthew 5:14-16 (NIV)*

It is time for God's children to shine brightly in this dark world. We are called to be a light in this dark world, stand out, and be different. The world needs to see something different about us.

I remember one December night when Adessa and I sat down to watch the Christmas Movie *"It's a Wonderful Life."* Suddenly, the power went out.

As we sat in the darkness, I thought about turning on our standby generator. Then it hit me: if we turn on the generator for water and heat, our Christmas lights will turn on automatically. While every other house on the street will be dark, our yard will be lit like the house in *Deck the Halls.* (Maybe they will even see it from space.) It would definitely stand out and show a distinction.

God calls us to stand out like Christmas lights during a blackout.

• When the world says, *"Blend in,"* the Bible says, *"Come apart and be separate."*

• When the world says *"Bow,"* the Bible says, *"Stand firm in the faith."*

• When the world says, *"Embrace the darkness,"* Jesus tells us to be a light in the dark world.

This is what it means to influence the world instead of allowing the world to influence us.

3. We are to be messengers to the lost.

Jesus' last words to us before He returned to Heaven was a command to be spiritual influencers.

> **Jesus came to them and said, "All authority in Heaven and on earth has been given to me. Therefore go and make disciples of all nations, baptizing them in the name of the Father and of the Son and of the Holy Spirit, and teaching them to obey everything I have commanded you. And surely I am with you always, to the very end of the age." -Matthew 28:18-19 (NIV)**

These verses are called *The Great Commission*, but too many of God's people treat them like it's the great option. But Jesus doesn't say, *"If you feel like it,"* or *"If it doesn't make too much trouble, cause too many waves, or upset too many people..."* No, He says, **"GO!"**

The Greek word used here for go is *"poreuomai."* It is an action verb. It means *"to depart, travel, take action."*[3]

This is a call to action for a believer. What are we called to do? The message is quite clear. Make disciples. Influence their lives. Teach them to live for God's kingdom.

A man who influences the world leads people to God and His kingdom.

4. We are to be different from the world.

The Bible repeatedly calls us to be influencers in the world around us. It tells us to stop letting the world influence how we think and act and start influencing the world. Look at these passages:

> *Do not be unequally yoked with unbelievers. For what partnership has righteousness with lawlessness? Or what fellowship has light with darkness? What accord has Christ with Belial? Or what portion does a believer share with an unbeliever? What agreement has the temple of God with idols? For we are the temple of the living God; as God said,*
>
> *"I will make my dwelling among them and walk among them, and I will be their God, and they shall be my people.*
>
> *Therefore go out from their midst, and be separate from them, says the Lord, and touch no unclean thing;*
>
> *then I will welcome you, and I will be a father to you, and you shall be sons and daughters to me, says the Lord Almighty." -2 Corinthians 6:14-18*

These verses show us how to live and influence the world. I love how the Message translation states these verses.

> *Don't become partners with those who reject God. How can you make a partnership out of right and wrong? That's not partnership; that's war. Is light best friends with dark? Does Christ go strolling with the Devil? Do trust and mistrust hold hands? Who would think of setting up pagan idols in God's holy Temple? But that is exactly what we are, each of us a temple in whom God lives. God himself put it this way:*
>
> *"I'll live in them, move into them; I'll be their God and they'll be my people.*

*So leave the corruption and compromise; leave it for good,"
says God.*

*"Don't link up with those who will pollute you. I want you
all for myself.*

I'll be a Father to you; you'll be sons and daughters to me."

*The Word of the Master, God. -2 Corinthians 6:14-18
(MSG)*

The Message makes the idea of partnering or embracing the ways of the world an unfathomable concept. It is seen as an impossibility.

In these verses, the Bible tells us the importance of coming apart and being separate, giving us some examples of specific ways to do it.

We are not to be influenced by the world. Look at all of the examples in these passages saying that we can't combine the Spirit of God and lusting after the spirit of the world. We can't have the Holy Spirit inside of us and worship idols. We can't have the Holy Spirit inside of us and also envy those living immoral lives.

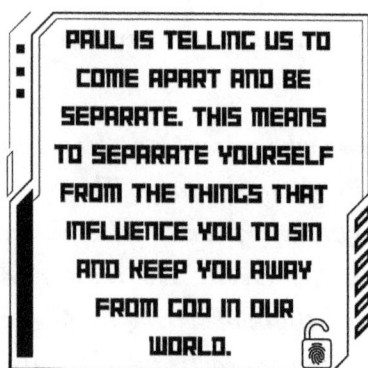

> PAUL IS TELLING US TO COME APART AND BE SEPARATE. THIS MEANS TO SEPARATE YOURSELF FROM THE THINGS THAT INFLUENCE YOU TO SIN AND KEEP YOU AWAY FROM GOD IN OUR WORLD.

Paul is telling us to come apart and be separate. This means to separate yourself from the things that influence you to sin and keep you away from God in our world.

It's harder to be separate than ever because so many things always want to influence us. We carry our phones around with us constantly, and the whole world is available to us there. We hear messages coming through social media wanting to influence us away from God. There are messages on the TV, in movies, radio, and in every avenue trying to pull us away from God's ways and to follow the practices of a secular society.

We have friends and people around us who are also trying to pull us in those directions. As men of God, we must say, *"No, I'm not going to let these things influence me."* If we cannot stand against the influence, the Bible tells us that we must do away with those things.

You cannot yoke yourself with things that influence you to do evil. Paul warns us about being influenced. But that's not the only reason the Bible tells us to be separate and different. It's also so that we can be an influence.

As mentioned in this chapter, we are to be the light. We are to be the salt. We are to be the ones to take a stand, raise the standard, and say, *"I live by God's ways. I live differently."*

We are to be the ones influencing other people to stop and think, *"I want to be like that."* We can't do that if we have blended ourselves together with the world.

The world must not influence us. We need to be influencing the world. When we live differently from the world, people notice.

- When we respond in love rather than anger.

- When we refuse to participate in immoral behavior.

- When we choose integrity over lies.

- When we treat all women with respect rather than viewing them as sexual objects.

- When we handle money wisely.

- When we show love and grace instead of anger or abuse.

The list could go on and on. People will notice the difference when we live like Jesus, following the principles of God's Word.

It allows us to answer, *"Why do you do that?"*

Then, we can share the Gospel.

When we live differently, it triggers interest. That interest may inspire others. It influences them to seek God, live by Biblical truth, or even make better life choices.

Think about it: How often has someone influenced you because they stood out?

Did they inspire you to try harder, do better, and change your life?

I have been blessed to have such men in my life who influenced me at critical stages of my growth.

- In high school, I had a friend named Ryan who showed me it was good to be interested in spiritual things and to be a good guy.

- In college, I had a professor named Daniel who demonstrated to me what it meant to be a true man of God, something I had never experienced growing up.

- In my early ministry, I had a friend named Tom who encouraged me that I could do anything for God's Kingdom that I set my heart to do.

- I had another friend named Tom who loved me enough to be hard on me and whip me into shape so I could be an even more effective man and spiritual leader.

These men influenced my life, and in turn, I like to think I am now influencing the lives of other men. I know I am shining a bright light into the darkness, refusing to dim the light or weaken my bold walk with God.

Are you influencing others around you toward God? How bright is your light shining? Are you resisting the temptation to dim the light so as not to offend others?

Are you still salty? Is your life making others thirsty to know God?

Are you fulfilling your Great Commission to reach the lost and bring them into the kingdom?

God is calling all of us to be men who stand out as godly men so that others around us will notice, be influenced, and say, *"I want to be more like him."* It is indeed our calling, our Great Commission. It's how we build our Father's kingdom. It's who we are, influencers changing the world one life at a time.

Group Study Questions:

1. What's your favorite thing to put on french fries?

2. Who has been a positive influence on your life spiritually?

3. Are you influencing others around you toward God?

4. How bright is your light shining? Are you resisting the temptation to dim the light so as not to offend others?

5. Are you still salty? Is your life making others thirsty to know God?

6. Are you fulfilling your Great Commission to reach the lost and bring them into the kingdom?

7. How has the world been influencing you in the wrong way? How can you stop this influence?

8. After reading this chapter, what is one thing you will put into practice or one thing you will change in your life?

9. How can we, as a group, help you do this?

CHAPTER TWELVE
IT'S WHAT WE DO

Guys, we have reached the end of our time together on this journey. I hope this book has helped you realize who you really are. I hope you have grasped your true identity as God's sons and are embracing the freedom that comes with this truth.

I hope you have realized that:

- You are victorious in God, not victims of the world.

- You are a warrior who stands up for God and those He entrusted to you.

- You are the adopted son of the most high God.

- You don't just hear God's Word; you do what it says.

- You are a leader in the world, not a ruler or dictator.

- You have the ability and call to live a pure and holy life before God.

- You are committed to following God instead of just being His number-one fan.

- You are a created being, designed for a specific purpose.

- You are called to coach the next generation and free them to grow spiritually.

- You are called to influence the world and lead them to God.

This is who you are! It's your nature, your call, your purpose. It is what God has empowered you to be.

However, there is one last thing to discuss in this book. In the words of Uncle Ben In Spiderman, *"With great power comes great responsibility."*[1]

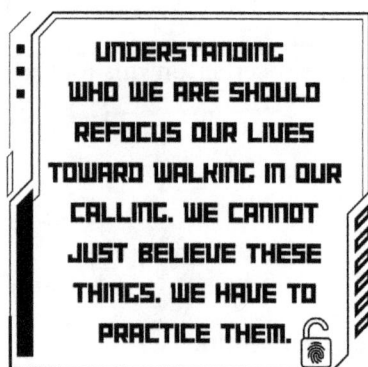

UNDERSTANDING WHO WE ARE SHOULD REFOCUS OUR LIVES TOWARD WALKING IN OUR CALLING. WE CANNOT JUST BELIEVE THESE THINGS. WE HAVE TO PRACTICE THEM.

We are responsible for knowing and understanding these things and allowing them to change how we think and act. This knowledge should refocus our lives toward walking in our calling. We cannot just believe these things. We have to practice them.

What does it profit, my brethren, if someone says he has faith but does not have works? Can faith save him? If a brother or sister is naked and destitute of daily food, and one of you says to them, "Depart in peace, be warmed and filled," but you do not give them the things which are needed for the body, what does it profit? Thus also faith by itself, if it does not have works, is dead. -James 2:14-17 (NKJV)

I like how the Message states verse 14:

Isn't it obvious that God-talk without God-acts is outrageous nonsense? -James 2:17 (MSG)

Martin Luther is quoted as saying:

"A person is justified [made right with God] by faith alone but not by a faith that is alone."[2]

The knowledge you have obtained about who you really are and how God sees you should spur you on to more spiritual growth. It should affect every area of your life. It should change how you view life, yourself, and your walk with God. But it should also spur you into action.

It should make you desire more of God and less of the world. It should cause a deeper hunger for the Word of God. You should be a more effective husband, father, son, brother, friend, and Christian.

That is why we have created this year's daily Bible plan to accompany this book. It is titled *It's What We Do*. Each of the 52 weekly devotionals focuses on actions that should be a part of every man of God's life. I encourage you to take advantage of this resource and to begin incorporating these actions and attitudes into your life.

As we end our time together, I want to pray for you.

Dear Heavenly Father, I thank you for my brother in Christ, who has read and completed this book. Please continue to help him grow and walk in his identity. Give Him strength, perseverance, and resolve to stand firm against the lies of the world trying to redefine manhood. Help him resist the calls to change his masculine identity and help him never bow to society.

Give him the boldness to be a shining light to the world, to live a light that shows the world what it means to be a man of God. Help him resist temptation, never bow, never blend, and never bend. Help him walk in the knowledge of who he is in You. In Jesus, Name, Amen!

Group Study Questions:

1. What chapter stood out to you the most as an area you need to work harder in knowing and living your true identity?

2. Why is it important to know who we are regarding what we do?

3. Martin Luther said, *"A person is justified [made right with God] by faith alone but not by a faith that is alone."* What do you think he meant?

4. Will you commit to using the **It's What We Do Daily Bible Plan**?

5. After reading this chapter, what is one thing you will put into practice or one thing you will change in your life?

6. How can we, as a group, help you do this?

IT'S WHO WE ARE WORKBOOK

Chapter One:

Write your own definition of identity:

Write your plan of how you will approach this study, ie., what day/time will you do the reading etc., so you are prepared for your weekly men's group?

Contract Between You and God

(and your men's group)

Will you commit to:

Reading each chapter, including Scripture verses? Yes/No

Sincerely examine your heart using the questions at the end of each chapter. Yes/No

Openly discuss the chapter with the men in your group with honesty and vulnerability. Yes/No

I, _____, am committed to understanding my true identity as a man of God and becoming everything God created me to be. I affirm this decision with my signature.

_____   _____
            (Sign)   (Date)

Group Study Questions:

1. What podcasts do you listen to?

2. Why is it important to know your identity in Christ?

3. How is the world distorting men's identities today?

4. Why is it important to understand the power available to us as God's sons?

5. What does the privilege of being God's sons mean to you on a daily basis?

6. How does the idea of God's protection enable us to walk in our true calling?

7. After reading this chapter, what is one thing you will put into practice or one thing you will change in your life?

8. How can we, as a group, help you do this?

Chapter Two:

How do you believe the world was created? Write it down here:

Write down four ways God's views on manhood differ from the world's views:

1.

2.

3.

4.

Write down your purpose in life and three ways actions you can take to grow in this purpose:

Description:

1.

2.

3.

Group Study Questions:

1. Who is your favorite superhero?

2. Why is it essential to believe that God created everything?

3. Why is it important to understand Biblical manhood since society wants to promote gender neutrality?

4. This chapter states, *"God created you for a specific reason with a specific purpose. Our job as God's men is to find out what that purpose is and do it with every ounce of passion we have!"* What does this mean to you?

5. Have you discovered your purpose? How are you walking in this purpose?

6. After reading this chapter, what is one thing you will put into practice or one thing you will change in your life?

7. How can we, as a group, help you do this?

Chapter Three:

Write down the difference between being an heir and a slave.

What are three changes you need to make to live a life worthy of your calling?

1.

2.

3.

What keeps you from running to God in times of need? Write it down, then ask God to forgive you.

Group Study Questions:

1. Can you remember a time when you were young when something went wrong, and you had to get an adult to help? Tell this story.

2. How does the truth that God is your father make you feel?

3. This chapter states, *"Someone who loves God and is grateful to Him for saving him and setting him free will express their gratitude by living differently than the world."* How can you personally express this gratitude to God? What steps can you take?

4. Are you doing everything possible to live a life worthy of your calling as heirs? What changes do you need to make?

5. Do you see God as an angry father waiting to punish or a loving father waiting to forgive and welcome you back? What thinking do you need to change?

6. After reading this chapter, what is one thing you will put into practice or one thing you will change in your life?

7. How can we, as a group, help you do this?

Chapter Four:

What is an area of sin that you need to deal with in your life? Write down a battle plan to gain victory:

What are three ways you can fight for your family?

1.

2.

3.

What are three ways you can stand against evil in today's culture?

1.

2.

3.

Group Study Questions:

1. Superman had many abilities, i.e., flying, X-ray vision, super strength, etc. What power of Superman do you wish you had?

2. What does it mean to be a *"peaceful warrior"*?

3. Why is it vital for us to remember that we are fighting against evil and demonic dark forces, not our fellow men?

4. What areas of sin have you been entertaining? How can you get brutal with it and destroy it?

5. How does being a peaceful warrior relate to our families?

6. Do you fight for Biblical truth? What are some ways you can do this in life?

7. Do you blend in with culture or bend to pressure? How can you begin to stand in the gap against the evil in society?

8. After reading this chapter, what is one thing you will put into practice or one thing you will change in your life?

9. How can we, as a group, help you do this?

Chapter Five:

Have there been areas where you act like a dictator, not a leader? Write it down below.

List four practical steps you can take to make changes. What can you do differently? What do you need to start doing? What needs to stop?

1.

2.

3.

4.

Make a list of who you need to ask to forgive you. Be specific in what you need to ask.

Group Study Questions:

1. What does being *"the boss"* mean to you?

2. This chapter stated, *"God's design was for men to be leaders, not rulers, servants, not dictators."* What does this mean?

3. Do you serve your family or expect to be served?

4. This chapter states, *"Jesus washed feet. The least we can do is wash a few dirty dishes."* What does this mean, and how can you apply it to your family?

5. What steps must you take to change if you struggle with being a dictator instead of a leader?

6. After reading this chapter, what is one thing you will put into practice or one thing you will change in your life?

7. How can we, as a group, help you do this?

Chapter Six:

Are you making excuses for anything in your life that is causing you to live an impure life, i.e., tv shows, movies, websites?   List them below.

Write down three steps you are going to take to gain victory:

1.

2.

3.

Write down three people you would feel comfortable asking to be an accountability partner.

1.

2.

3.

Group Study Questions:

1. Is there anything you're allergic to, like smoke?

2. This chapter states, *"We cannot have a proper relationship with God if we reject purity and embrace sexual impurity."* Why is this true?

3. Do you change the channel when you see an unmarried couple in bed canoodling together on TV?

4. Do you leave a conversation at work or with friends when the coarse jokes or sexual innuendos start flying?

5. Do people around you know better than to have off-color conversations around you?

6. Have you been guilty of blaming women for your sexual issues? If so, have you repented?

7. Do you have an accountability partner? If not, will you commit to finding one?

8. After reading this chapter, what is one thing you will put into practice or one thing you will change in your life?

9. How can we, as a group, help you do this?

Chapter Seven:

Write down three things that stood out to you the most in this chapter:

1.

2.

3.

Write down three actions you can take to apply these in your life:

1.

2.

3.

Group Study Questions:

1. What's your favorite Christmas movie?

2. What's the difference between a follower and a fan?

3. Have you ever been guilty of being more of a fan of God than a follower?

4. What steps can you take to move from fandom to following?

5. This chapter states: *"We need to decide every day to be a follower, deny ourselves and our desires, go wherever God wants us to go, or do whatever He wants us to do."* What are practical ways of doing this?

6. After reading this chapter, what is one thing you will put into practice or one thing you will change in your life?

7. How can we, as a group, help you do this?

Chapter Eight:

Have you ever felt like the victim? Write down the memory.

What are three steps you can take to overcome this victim mentality?

1.

2.

3.

Group Study Questions:

1. When you were a kid, what did you want to be when you grew up?

2. What does it mean to be a victim?

3. Have you struggled with feeling like a victim? In what ways?

4. This chapter states, *"A victim mentality...has no place in the life of a believer. Victimhood is the state of powerlessness, but we are filled with the power of the Holy Spirit!"* What does this mean practically?

5. Do you want to stop being a victim? No matter the cost?

6. How does reading the Bible help us overcome being a victim?

7. After reading this chapter, what is one thing you will put into practice or one thing you will change in your life?

8. How can we, as a group, help you do this?

Chapter Nine:

Write down four steps you can implement to practice being a doer:

1.

2.

3.

4.

Write down an action plan of when and how you will spend time in the Bible.

Group Study Questions:

1. Have you ever spilled paint on a valuable surface? What did you do to fix the mess?

2. Do you spend time daily in God's Word?

3. This chapter states, *"Our calling is to let the Word of God change us, make us into new, sanctified believers, and grow into spiritual warriors."* How can you begin to do this?

4. Do you take notes in church?

5. How often do you consciously decide to make a change after hearing a sermon?

6. Is your life built on hearing AND OBEYING the Word of God?

7. After reading this chapter, what is one thing you will put into practice or one thing you will change in your life?

8. How can we, as a group, help you do this?

Chapter Ten:

What can you do to help a younger man succeed in God's kingdom?

List five ways you can pray for the younger man you're mentoring.

1.

2.

3.

4.

5.

Group Study Questions:

1. Who is your favorite quarterback of all time?

2. What are some ways you can help your younger teammates succeed?

3. What is one lesson you can teach a younger man to help him succeed in God's kingdom?

4. What prayers can you pray for a younger man?

5. What does this phrase mean to you: *"A real man of God realizes his true calling in life is not to build kingdoms; it is to train kings!"*

6. After reading this chapter, what is one thing you will put into practice or one thing you will change in your life?

7. How can we, as a group, help you do this?

Chapter Eleven:

Write down your testimony so you are prepared if you have a chance to share it with someone:

Write down four ways you can practically be salt and light:

1.

2.

3.

4.

Group Study Questions:

1. What's your favorite thing to put on french fries?

2. Who has been a positive influence on your life spiritually?

3. Are you influencing others around you toward God?

4. How bright is your light shining? Are you resisting the temptation to dim the light so as not to offend others?

5. Are you still salty? Is your life making others thirsty to know God?

6. Are you fulfilling your Great Commission to reach the lost and bring them into the kingdom?

7. How has the world been influencing you in the wrong way? How can you stop this influence?

8. After reading this chapter, what is one thing you will put into practice or one thing you will change in your life?

9. How can we, as a group, help you do this?

Chapter Twelve:

What were your three biggest takeaways from this study?

1.

2.

3.

What are three actions you are committed to taking or changes you are committed to making after reading this book?

1.

2.

3.

A personal note from Jamie:

I believe in you. I believe that you have what it takes to walk in your calling as a man of God. I believe that you have the strength to do whatever God asks of you, to go wherever He leads, and to stand firm against anything and everything the world throws at you. You have what it takes to follow God, to pick up your cross, to follow God no matter what! God can use you and inspire another man to do the same. You have what it takes! It's who you are!

-Jamie Holden

Will you accept the challenge of this book?

If so, state so below:

I, _____ declare today that I will embrace and walk in my identity as a man of God. I will obediently follow Him as I work to fulfill His purpose for my life. I will overcome whatever personality traits or weaknesses I have. I will follow Him in faith, resolving to stand firm. No matter what the world or the enemy throws at me or what discouragement I will face, I will persevere. Even if it brings persecution, I will be grateful to God and wholeheartedly serve Him. I will read and obey His Word, allowing the Bible to convict me and lead me to make changes in my life. God has called me to be a light to dark world, and today I choose to answer His call!

_____   _____

Signature   Date

Group Study Questions:

1. What chapter stood out to you the most as an area you need to work harder in knowing and living your true identity?

2. Why is it important to know who we are regarding what we do?

3. Martin Luther said, *"A person is justified [made right with God] by faith alone but not by a faith that is alone."* What do you think he meant?

4. Will you commit to using the *It's What We Do Daily Bible Plan?*

5. After reading this chapter, what is one thing you will put into practice or one thing you will change in your life?

6. How can we, as a group, help you do this?

BIBLIOGRAPHY

Chapter 1

1. Fishel, Danielle, Friedle, Will, Rider, Strong, host. *"Adam Scott Meets World."* Pod Meets World, 23-1-2023, https://podcasts.apple.com/us/podcast/adam-scott-meets-world/id1629908611?i=1000595997409.

Chapter 2

1. Assemblies of God Positions Paper *"The Doctrine of Creation"* (ADOPTED BY THE GENERAL PRESBYTERY IN SESSION AUGUST 20, 2010)", website: https://ag.org/Beliefs/Position-Papers/The-Doctrine-of-Creation

2. *"toxic."* Merriam-Webster.com. Merriam-Webster, 2011. Web. 20 July 2023.

3. Casarella, Jennifer M.D, *"Toxic Person: Signs to Look For."* *WebMD*, 18 December, 2022, www.webmd.com/mental-health/signs-toxic-person. Accessed 27 July 2023.

Chapter 3

1. Brewer , Jack . *"Issue Brief: Fatherlessness and It's Effects On American Society."* *America First Policy,* 15 May 2023, americafirstpolicy.com/latest/issue-brief-fatherlessness-and-its-effects-on-american-society#:~:text=ISSUE%20BRIEF:%20Fatherlessness%20and%20its%20effects%20on%20American%20society,-May%2015,%202023&text=Across%20America,%202022%20data%20indicates,are%20led%20by%20single%20mothers. Accessed 21 Jul. 2023.

Chapter 5

1. *Shiny, Happy People: Duggar Family Secrets.* Directed by Julia Willoughby Nason and Oliva Crist , performances by Jill Duggar, Amazon Studio, 2023.

Chapter 6

1. God Rules.NET - *Bible Study Tools, Bible Commentary Library & More*, godrules.net/library/strongs2b/gre53.htm. Accessed 27 July 2023.

2. Barnes, Albert . *Barnes' Notes on the New Testament.* Kregel Publications, 1962. p. 1049.

Chapter 7

1. *White Christmas.* Directed by Michael Kurtiz, performances by Bing Crosby, et al., Paramount Pictures, 1954.

Chapter 9

1. Patrick, Dan, host and producer. *The Dan Patrick Show,* 16-6-2023, https://omny.fm/shows/the-dan-patrick-show/playlists/podcast

2. Donald C Stamps, Study Notes on James 2, *Fire Bible: English Standard Version,* (Peabody, MA: Henderickson Publishers Marketing, LLC, 2014), Pg 2171.

3. Earls, Aaron. LifeWay Research. *"State of the Bible"* (January 19, 2020) https://research.lifeway.com/2021/05/28/more-americans-are-reading-the-bible-now-what#:~:text=Close%20to%20a%20third%20 Accessed: 27 July 2023.

4.   Steinbuch, Yaron. *US Religious Sermons Ranked by Length, Commonly Used Words in New Study."* New York Post,   https://nypost.com/2019/12/16/us-religious-sermons-ranked-by-length-commonly-used-words-in-new-study//. Accessed 27-7-2023.

Chapter 11

1.   Min, Sarah. *"86% of Young Americans Want to Become a Social Media Influencer."Money Watch*, 25 July. 2023,https://www.cbsnews.com/news/social-media-influencers-86-of-young-americans-want-to-become-one/   .

2.   Donald C Stamps, Study Notes on Matthew 5, *Fire Bible: English Standard Version,* (Peabody, MA: Henderickson Publishers Marketing, LLC, 2014), Pg 1522.

3.   God Rules.NET - *Bible Study Tools, Bible Commentary Library & More*, godrules.net/library/strongs2b/gre4198.htm. Accessed 27 July 2023.

Chapter 12

1. *Spider-Man*. Directed by Sam Raimi, performances by Toby Maguire , et al., Columbia Pictures, Marvel Enterprises, Laura Ziskin Productions, 2002.

2. Donald C Stamps, Study Notes on James 1, *Fire Bible: English Standard Version,* (Peabody, MA: Henderickson Publishers Marketing, LLC, 2014), Pg 2173.

Also Available

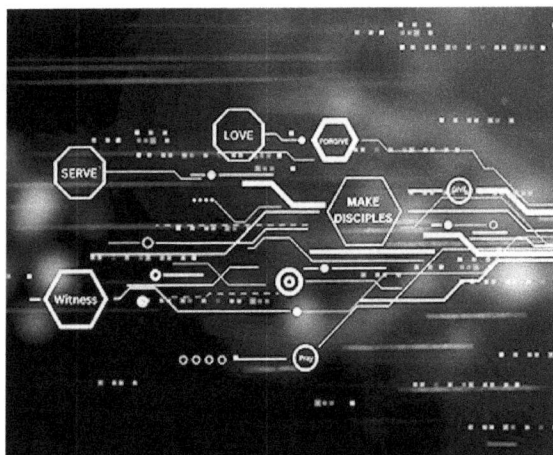

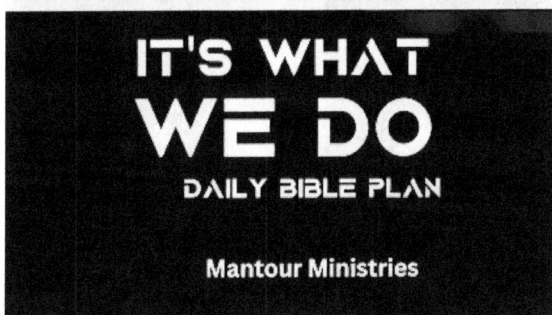

The actions we take define us.
IT'S WHAT WE DO DAILY BIBLE PLAN

For more information, visit:
www.mantourministries.com/Bibleplan

ALSO AVAILABLE FROM MANTOUR MINISTRIES

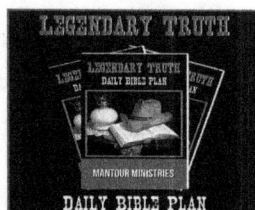

Jamie loves to speak to men and is available to speak at your next men's event. Jamie combines humor and his personal testimony to both engage and challenge men to grow in their walk with God. He uses his testimony of overcoming abuse as well as dealing with his physical and emotional issues growing up to encourage men that no matter what their background or where they have come from in life, they can grow into mighty men in God's kingdom.

"Years ago, while I was attending the University of Valley Forge, God gave me a deep desire to minister to men. My calling is to help men learn what it means to be a godly man and how to develop a deep, personal relationship with their heavenly Father. We strive to challenge and encourage men to reach their full potential in God's kingdom."

If you are interested in having Jamie at your next men's event as a speaker or workshop leader, or if you are interested in having him come share with your church, contact him by visiting www.mantourministries.com/invitejamie. He is also available to speak for one or multiple weeks on the theme of his books, Legendary Grit, Ride or Die, Burning Daylight, Whatever It Takes, Invincible: Scaling The Mountains That Keep Us From Victory. Putting On Manhood, Legacy: Living a Life that Lasts, and Get in the Game.

JAMIE HOLDEN

FOUNDER/DIRECTOR, MANTOUR MINISTRIES

SCAN WITH PHONE CAMERA

GIVE ONLINE AT
HTTPS://WWW.MANTOURMINISTRIES.COM/PARTNER

www.ingramcontent.com/pod-product-compliance
Lightning Source LLC
Chambersburg PA
CBHW070041100426
42740CB00013B/2751